# Lazaris...

Lazaris says he came not as a guru, b[...]
I value most I've learned from friends, and [...]
have.
— *Colin Higgins, Writer/Director, H[...]
Play, The Best Little Whorehouse in Texas,*

I have been seriously investigating this field for over five years and have talked to several hundred people who claim to channel — and have found Lazaris to be one of the select few who are wise and empowering. Lazaris adds a very much needed credibility to this entire field. I especially appreciate Lazaris' consistent and unique emphasis on providing tools by which we can discover our own truths, our own strengths, and our own power.
— *Jon Klimo, Author of* **Channeling: Investigations**, *former professor, Rutgers University*

Lazaris is the friend we always wish for, and now he's here for everyone. We had a good relationship before, but he showed us how to love each other even more. We always thought that success came after long and hard work. Lazaris taught us it's more fun to do it quicker and easier. With Lazaris' love and help we have created one miracle after another.
— *Renee Taylor & Joe Bologna, Actors, Writers & Directors*

With wisdom, compassion and marvelous humor, Lazaris, from his greater perspective outside our "Set," makes vividly clear how physical reality works. He knows me absolutely and is there for me — even when I am not! Thank you, Lazaris. I love you. . . .
— *Betty Fuller, Director, The Trager Institute*

I went to Lazaris' first public channeling in 1979. Since that day the quality of information and communication has always expanded and surpassed itself. The growth I have made because of our friendship has brought me into the New Age with clarity and assurance. I love Lazaris even more today and rejoice in our shared vision for the exciting future!
— *Nicholas Eliopoulos, Producer, Director, Writer, Emmy Award-winning Editor for "Wallenberg: A Hero's Story," Senior Vice President of Development/Production, The Don Johnson Company*

There is channeling, and then there is Lazaris. . . .

# Who is Lazaris?

Lazaris is a non-physical entity. He is a consciousness without form — a Spark of Light, a Spark of Love — an energy that has never chosen to take human form. He is most frequently known as "the one who waits for us at the edge of our reality."

Lazaris is wise beyond what we have known, loving beyond what we have conceived, and committed to each of us in our search for enlightenment. He is a delightful friend — a gentle and powerful guide for our Spiritual Journey Home to God/Goddess/All That Is.

The way that Lazaris communicates to us is called channeling — in this case Objective, Full-Trance Channeling. That means several things. "Objective" means that Lazaris is not a part of the consciousness of his channel. "Full Trance" means that the channel is not aware of what is being said during the trance state. "Channeling" is perhaps best described by Lazaris directly:

*"In order to communicate with you, we send forth a series of vibrations. These vibratory frequencies go through a series of "step-down generations" until they can safely enter your reality.*

*"The energy field of the one you call Jach acts like an antenna; his body, like an amplifier. The vibration we create in our reality is thus amplified in your reality. Your ears and eyes pick up those amplified frequencies and translate them into sounds — you hear a voice — and pictures — you see animation.*

*"When we communicate we are not in the body — how archaic! Such behavior is no more necessary than having your nightly newscaster actually be in your television set!*

*"We keep the channel in a sleep-like state so that he stays out of the way. It would be possible for him to "witness" what we say — to "listen" as the vibrations go by — but we prefer him to be completely out of the way. The best way to keep the information pure is to have the channel be as much a 'pure instrument' as possible."*

Lazaris is a channeled entity, but he is so very much more. Many who are familiar with metaphysics and channeling say, "There is channeling, and then there is Lazaris. He is so far beyond . . . he stands alone in this field."

# The Sacred Journey:
# You and Your Higher Self

Concept: Synergy Publishing

Concept: Synergy Publishing

# *Lazaris*
## *The Sacred Journey:  You and Your Higher Self*

1st Printing, 1987

Published by Concept: Synergy Publishing
279 S. Beverly Drive, Suite 604
Beverly Hills, CA 90212
213/285-1507, 714/337-0789

Cover painting, "The Sacred Journey," © 1987 by Gilbert Williams,
Courtesy of Isis Unlimited, One Rodeo Drive, 201 N. Rodeo Drive,
Beverly Hills, CA 90210, 213/858-0290.

ISBN 1-55638-080-1
Library of Congress Catalog Card Number: 87-091323

Printed in the United States of America

10 9 8 7 6 5 4 3 2 1

# Dedication

*This book is dedicated to Peny,
the one we came to touch, the one who truly touches us.
We love you,*

*—Lazaris*

# *Other Books by Lazaris*

Lazaris: A Spark of Love

# Table of Contents

## Introductions

## Part I: The Journey Begins

## Part II: The Four Choices To Grow

## Part III: The Steps of Getting There

## Part IV: You and Your Higher Self

## Appendix

# INTRODUCTION

## by Jach Pursel

Afraid, I just walked. I didn't know what else to do. Somehow moving seemed to help. I told myself: "Keep moving, just keep moving, Jach, and somehow everything will be all right." There was no logic in that spontaneous mantra, but then there was no logic in most of what had been happening to me over the past several weeks.

"Keep moving, just keep moving . . ." At first, I thought it would just go away. I hoped it would just go away. I also hoped my hope would be enough so that nothing would come of it. But I heard the voice. I did hear the voice. I could not deny it any longer. The lack of denial did nothing to help me understand, so I just kept moving and repeating my private mantra. I was scared. I was terrified.

"When had it all begun?" I heard myself ask. This was a stalling tactic for sure, but I followed the question. I had nowhere else to go.

I'm not sure when it began. It seemed so simple then. I was on a business trip. I was at the Home Office, and it was half-way through a five-day conference/training session. Young execs from all over the country were there. I hated being away from home. These trips were considered a "perk" of mid-management, but I never felt very perky.

I don't know why I decided to meditate that evening. I had learned "how" to meditate at a course Peny had dragged me to back in 1972. The course had promised great results, which she found plausible and exciting. I found the claims unbelievable. She was right.

For me, meditation was a euphemism for napping. I would — how do they say it? — I would go "too deep" in almost all of my meditations. Though I had learned it, and had seen other people have great results, I had all but dropped the practice. Glorified napping did not seem to be the "way home" for me, or the way anywhere for that matter! I don't know why I decided to meditate that evening.

My eyes closed, and I began my routine of breathing the tension out of my body. I could feel myself starting to slip off to sleep. Then something very strange happened. I started to visualize! I saw things! I saw things *spontaneously.* This was a first! The rapid-fire images culminated as I experienced this wonderful man standing in front of me. He was gentle. I was not afraid. He talked to me. I remembered every word.

I bolted. The meditation abruptly ended. I remembered every word! Writing furiously I had to capture the moment. Exhausted, I called Peny. She lifted her enthusiasm to match mine. I loved her for that.

Nothing happened after that. I had asked his name. Lazaris was the word I heard. I asked again thinking of "Lazarus" of the Bible, or the department store in Columbus. The name was distinct: L-A-Z-A-R-I-S. The emphasis was emphatically on the second syllable (LA-**ZAR**-IS). I had a name, but no further contact. I all but forgot about the whole experience.

October 3rd, 1974. Early evening. Sitting on the bed, plumped up in pillows, I am preparing to meditate (ha!). I am going to seek insight (ha!) to help guide our lives. Things were not really so bad as to warrant such extreme measures! Yet over the fourteen years of our being together, I had learned to pay attention to Peny's psychic flashes and intuitive gestalts. She had "flashed" that I should do a meditation.

She asked me questions. I answered. The questions were great. The answers were boring. Maybe that's why I fell asleep. I thought I had fallen asleep. I could feel myself drifting away. I tried to stay awake. I tried to hold onto the sound of her voice, but the soft lure of sleep won out. I drifted off. I was asleep.

Two hours later, Peny didn't hear my sheepish apology for having dozed off. She was excitedly tumbling over words trying to tell me that an entity had spoken through me. She thought I had fallen asleep again, too. This time, however, my head didn't bob, so she waited. Some minutes passed, and then a deep, resonant voice began where mine had left off. The answers, however, were powerful, not of the caliber of mine. She listened. She wrote as fast as she could. She was like a child with Santa Claus — she didn't question it then, she just took all the information she could get. She would evaluate it later.

The entity explained that he was Lazaris!  Yes, the same one I had contacted so many months before.  That experience had been in preparation for this one, though neither Peny nor I would begin to understand what "this" was for many years to come.  Lazaris requested two weeks of our time to finalize the necessary adjustments so he could "channel" through me.  He provided Peny with a simple, but detailed, method I should use to enter trance more easily.  He assured her that this experience would never be detrimental, that although he had neither a body nor time, he appreciated that we did, and he would never abuse either.

More questions are answered.  I know Peny is telling me the truth, because she does not lie.  The information explodes in my mind.  I hear the words.  I know they are true.  I cannot believe what I am hearing.  The contradictions are lost in the sweet comfort of avoidance.  I just refused to talk about it.

Every evening I would sit and close my eyes and take an "after-dinner nap."  Every evening Peny would enthusiastically tell me all that had transpired.  I listened.  I smiled.  I avoided.

After the two weeks, the necessary adjustments were complete.  Peny had come to know and trust this entity that I wasn't even really admitting was there.  Everything at work was just fine.  Everything was just fine.  I continued to avoid.  Peny, aware of my usual way of handling things I didn't understand, handed me a cassette with one word: "Listen."

"Keep moving, just keep moving . . . "  I couldn't deny that something was happening.  Afraid, I just walked.  I cried.  I did not know what to do.  Peny knew me so well that she left me alone.  Her tenderness and compassion was so great that she knew when loving meant to leave me alone.  I walked.  I cried.  I had never been so scared in my twenty-seven years.  I had never been so frightened.  What was happening to me?

Months would pass, months filled with evaluating Lazaris with casual friends about whom I knew very little.  They would come and talk to Lazaris and then report their conclusions.  These were people I trusted who also had extensive backgrounds in this new-to-me field of metaphysics.  I would slip into "trance," both terrified that he would come through and terrified that he wouldn't be there.  Gathering the feedback, I concluded that something very real was happening.  Many more months would pass before I could accept Lazaris for who he really was.

Then I referred to him as "it," which I suppose is technically more correct since Lazaris is neither male or female.  As I have come to know Lazaris, I have come to know his love, his humor, his giving and caring.  I have come to know his commitment to me and to all the human beings who find him.  I have come to understand his dedication to honesty.  He has become a friend.

He has become *my* friend, my very best friend. He is no longer an "it." To me, Lazaris is a "he."

I kept moving. I just kept moving that day in mid-October, 1974, and everything did turn out just fine.

The initial friends of Lazaris began telling their friends, who told their friends, and . . . As their friendships with Lazaris grew, so did mine. Each day, each week, I grew to love him more.

I remember one evening in (I think) 1976. By then Lazaris was conducting workshops, and I was listening to a cassette of the most recent one. It was very late. Alone in the totally dark living room, I was lying on the floor just listening. It still amazed me that that voice was coming out of my body. I just listened.

I heard the words, but that late night, I heard something more. It was between the words. I heard the love. I could hear the concern and the compassion. Tears rolled down my cheeks. The tears turned to sobs. I could feel Lazaris filling the room. I could feel Lazaris filling me with his incredible love and his soothing peace. I could feel his smile.

Though I had known that Lazaris was real for almost two years, that night I was finally at peace. That night was special.

Between 1974 and 1985 thousands of people found their friendships with Lazaris. He speaks privately with people all over the world and works with thousands more in seminars and workshops. The demand has become so massive that in November, 1985, Lazaris agreed to make video tape recordings available. They now number in the double-digits, and the demand increases. It is now time for books.

As I look back, I wish we had kept better records. We don't have the original notes that Peny took that evening in October, 1974. We don't even know the time of day. I can't begin to remember the day or even the month when I first meditated and "accidentally" discovered Lazaris. When all this happened, we had no idea that it meant anything at all. We had no idea that the phenomenon would even reoccur. There was no reason to document what might have been a fluke. Perhaps if we had known . . . but this whole experience unfolded itself in front of us. Peny and I felt more like observers than participants.

Now Peny and Michaell and I still wait and watch to see where Lazaris' love leads him and us. The waiting and watching is exciting. We know that Lazaris knows where it all leads.

He is taking us Home. He has been called the Consummate Friend, and that he has been to me. In a metaphysical environment where approaches to

spirituality proliferate with varying shades of validity and integrity, I am glad
to have a friend like Lazaris.  I am glad I "kept moving, just kept moving"
that day so many years ago.

— Jach Pursel, Lazaris' Channel

# *A Note on Lazaris' Use of Language . . .*

*Throughout this book Lazaris refers to himself as "we." Ever since he began communicating with us in 1974, he has done that. Lazaris says that each of us has many "selves," but that right now we are experiencing them "one at a time," and thus refer to ourselves as "I". Lazaris has many selves as well — many selves in many dimensions — but experiences them all simultaneously, and therefore refers to himself as "we." It is not the use of the "royal we," but rather Lazaris' experience of his own reality. . . .*

*Also, often you will find that Lazaris will use a plural pronoun in a place you might expect to find a singular one. This is to avoid using the generic masculine pronouns which tend to make women feel as though they are not included in what is being said. To make certain they do know they are included, Lazaris often uses plural pronouns which, though "against the rules," are better aligned with what is true.*

# *INTRODUCTION*

## *by Lazaris*

Well . . . All right . . . It is a pleasure to be here and to be talking with you. It is a pleasure to write to you.

We are here because you invited us — you as an individual and you as a humankind. You decided to grow, and you asked for help. You invited us, and we are here. More precisely, we are here to remind you . . .

That pain and fear are not the only methods of growth, that you can more elegantly grow through joy and love . . .

That you do create your own reality . . . There is no fine print or exception . . .

That there is a God/Goddess/All That Is who loves you, who knows your name . . .

That you love — you love "good enough."

There is another, very personal reason we are here. We are here to talk with Peny. By amplifying through "the Channel" the thoughts we create, we can touch the one who is called Peny. That is our desire.

In our decision to communicate to your plane and with your planet, we watched and observed. In our watchings and observings, we found a most beautiful spark of consciousness, a most beautiful spark of love and light. We found a most wonderful spark filled with the most wonderful laughter. We found Peny.

We scanned her lifetimes, seeing that she was done, knowing that she could move on — yet she returned to do more on the physical plane. So many of you make the mistake of thinking that you have to be perfect or that you have to get "permission" before you can expand, before you can "grow" to the higher levels. That was not the case with Peny. She knew it was her choice. We knew why she was returning. Did she?

The answer was in the laughter. Within the laughter was the love.

We chose to look closer and, without interference, to help her grow, to help her accomplish the work she came to do. We know she can do it all on her own. She knows that, too. But then we have not come as guru or master; we have come as a friend. The closer we look, the more pleased we are with our choice. The closer we get, the more we are touched by her laughter and her special love. The more we touch.

Each night, as most of the world has slipped off to sleep, while the Channel sits in the usual chair with his eyes closed, his consciousness drifts off. Silence. We enter the body silently. Often, before we begin — before most would even know we are there — she says, "Hi, Lazaris, how are you?"

She knows the question has no meaning to us because we have no time, no space, no form. Habits live long in your world. We smile and say, "Fine, just fine," having come to understand this as an expected response. And our "time" together has begun.

We often begin by discussing the issues and questions that comprise the fabric of her life. We chat in the darkened room quietly. We laugh. She laughs.

Sometimes we will describe a different technique or take her on a new meditation to make the final adjustments before we introduce it in a workshop. Together we explore the deeper meanings and intricacies of reality creation. Together we spin realities and dreams.

One evening Peny asked us to write a book that was not just another book. We said yes.

This is our response.

Peny, we begin with a topic that many might think is where we should end. We begin with *The Sacred Journey: You and Your Higher Self* because the key to your spirituality is your personal relationship with a very real God/Goddess/All That Is. Your Sacred Journey is the backbone of that relationship.

We begin with this skeleton and from "time to time" we will add layer after layer of information and understanding as well as specific techniques to help you become fully alive in the body of your spirituality.

We are not your guru or master.  We have long since moved beyond those levels.  We are your friend, and we love you, Peny.  As a friend, we are committed to you, and to your growth.  However long you decide you want to take, we will be here waiting for you at the edge of your reality.

You asked us to write a book that was not just another book.  This book is our answer to you.  It is more than a book . . . it is the beginning of a very long letter!

We love you, Peny.  With Love and Peace.

*— Lazaris*

# Introduction
## by Peny Prestini

Autumn, 1987

When Lazaris asked me to write an introduction for his book, I felt so deeply honored, and at the same time, so challenged about how to convey the warmth, the generosity, the excitement and the sense of wonder he brings to our everyday life.

"Just tell them what it's like to be with us," Lazaris said. "They want to see the personal side."

My relationship with Lazaris has been continually amazing for me because I can tangibly feel the depth and magnitude of his love, and I can actually see the significant results with myself, and so many others. . . . I can watch the solid consistency and the everpresent quality of his unconditional love grow even more vivid as the years with him roll by. In other words, I have come to realize that I can trust him completely, and therein lies a powerful healing and a life-changing opportunity.

The historical significance of what is unfolding before us with Lazaris is still far beyond our range of vision, but the excitement of the process of its discovery is a first-class adventure story. For so very many of us, it is what we have been waiting for.

While I was working on this introduction, something happened that threw me off-kilter. Sharing this process will certainly give you a glimpse into our private world and, as always, the teaching Lazaris helped me with has universal applications.

A good friend treated me very unfairly in her newly published book. Her action was imbalanced, inaccurate and patronizing; even when she apologized, I still felt betrayed. I knew I created my own reality — all of it — and my self-anger at allowing this mess rubbed salt into the pain of being carelessly hurt by someone I genuinely liked and trusted.

Friends called me as they read her book, upset and shocked by her conceit. I appreciated their empathy, but my focus seemed stuck on my sense of failure at having given myself such a raw deal. I felt betrayed by myself and increasingly wary of myself — I knew I needed to understand why I had created/allowed this in order to trust myself again. I turned to Lazaris for help.

While Jach went into trance, I painfully rolled my neck from side to side; I had managed to manifest TMJ and neck and shoulder pain on my left side. "How classic," I thought, "you're really going by the textbooks on this one."

As Lazaris greeted me, he reached for my hand and squeezed it, giving me a good-sized rose quartz sphere to hold while he did some Etheric Body energy work on me. Soon enough, I felt my muscles unclench and the pain recede. He worked quietly and patiently, attending not only to me, but to the three Himalayan cats competing for "his" (Jach's) lap; they react to Lazaris much like they do to a warm patch of sun on the carpet. The essence of what was happening between us washed over me, and I felt my perspective shifting and rising. At times like this, I can see so clearly and so far that nothing else matters.

"OK, Lazaris, I think I'm ready to work on it. Why on Earth did I create this?"

"Well, all right. First of all, you know we love you. And part of the reason that you created this is because of that fact. You feel guilty that we care as much as we do about you. You feel guilty because you don't know what you've done to deserve our love. Therefore, you open yourself up to these kinds of unfortunate situations. It's almost as if you think that 'since I have so much with Lazaris, I guess a little hurt and disappointment is the price I must pay.' So therefore, you allow things like this to occur. You see, there was nothing you did that caused this, but plenty that allowed it. Remember, you do create your own reality by either causing or allowing. You know the words, but you need to let in the meaning.

"Another reason: Sometimes you just feel guilty for being alive, for being happy and for being powerful. It's almost as if you wonder, 'What did I do to deserve all this?' Which brings us to the third reason that you created this reality.

"The third reason we call the "Catch-22" of deservability. The guilt produces a question of deservability, and the question of deservability produces a feeling of lack. The lack leads to doubt, and the doubt leads to feelings of undeservability. And then, as though in a spider web, you are caught: 'I created this because I don't think I deserve, and because I did create this, now I really don't deserve!' At least that's how the thinking goes.

"Because you feel so distrusting of yourself, it makes you feel even less deserving. 'After all,' you tell yourself, 'if I'd been deserving, I never would have let this happen in the first place.'"

"That's it, Lazaris, that's exactly how I feel."

"Exactly! And what you need to deal with now is the truth that you (and everyone else) are deserving just because you exist. That reason doesn't sound good enough to you. You see, you think that there's got to be a grander reason — a more important reason — to deserve, to deserve God's love. You look around for that grander reason, and you can't find it, and rather than realizing that you can't find it because it's not there — because it doesn't exist — you assume you can't find it because it's lacking in you."

"It's like I'm trying forever to earn something that I've already been given. It's like self-worth, right, Lazaris?"

"Absolutely so! Beautiful! The earning will drive you crazy. You simply have to accept that it is a given truth. So sometimes you'll create messes like this in order to try to get further insights into what's wrong with you, and there is nothing wrong with you! Nothing except the illusion of guilt and undeservability.

"Peny (he reached out to take my hand), it's important to understand: Life is a gift, and it is yours to learn how to receive, not to earn. Life is a gift, not a reward. You see?"

"I do, Lazaris. Thank you so much."

"But wait a moment — there's something more. We don't want you going away thinking that somehow you 'made' her do this, as though she were only a pawn in your game. She had her particular reasons for creating this reality. Her reasons were ones of 'cause' and yours were ones of 'allowing.' It just so happened that her reasons for creating this and yours for allowing this fit together as cogs in two wheels. Exactly why she created it is something she will have to look at someday. And she will. And the two of you will end up even closer for it."

We talked long into the night, analyzing aspects of life, exploring "beliefs" and "truths" and all sorts of systems, always with an eye out for limiting thoughts, always ready to soar too high rather than not high enough. We might have been in any time, the room lit by several vanilla-scented candles, the tables covered with crystals of every shape and hue. I felt outside of my self . . . aligned much more with Self. Michaell had joined us by now, and our discussion moved onto the field of metaphysics — my sense of disappointment in the carnival atmosphere sweetened by Lazaris' reminder of the essential purity of all people as they continue to seek union with God/Goddess/All That Is — the bittersweet determination that keeps us trying again and again, despite the confusion and charlatanism too frequently available.

Lazaris talked of the many books and projects he has plans for, of the work he is so gently doing, and a sense of profound humility and gratitude wrapped around Michaell and me as we looked at the years ahead.

It feels vulnerable to share this side of my life with you. People often write me that they love my laughter and humor on the "Evening with Lazaris and Peny" tapes, and I know I do feel more comfortable showing my ebullient side than this more serious side. And it's true that I can get in the place of worrying that you'll think it's unfair that I have this unique relationship with Lazaris. I used to want him not to talk about it. You can see the tell-tale tracks of undeservability . . .

Having more access to Lazaris only continually reaffirms my desire to share him with all of you. What other reaction could I have in the face of all that love?

Within weeks of knowing him (of course, he is not male — he is far beyond our concepts of gender), I began to realize the incredible importance of what he is . . . the magnitude of the opportunity we have with him.

Lazaris has never let me down. That sentence is staggering to me.

I am not finished yet with my personal grappling with guilt and deservability, but I can see the last few feet of the bridge now. I have Lazaris to thank for that. Thousands of you feel the same way, and I salute our kinship. I can see us all soaring and shining together in the new world he is guiding us toward, and my eyes fill with tears. He waits at the edge of our reality. He isn't going to ever let us down and, for me, that says it all.


I love you,


Peny
September, 1987
Los Angeles


PS: Lazaris and I want to acknowledge and thank Valerie Blalock, a Vice-President of Concept: Synergy, for her excellent help in editing this book and in facilitating its publishing process.

## Reference Sheets for Your Journey

*In the Appendix of this book are two sheets of paper which you may want to detach and use while you are reading the remainder of this book. Those pages outline the major components Lazaris will cover in the coming chapters, and can be used as a quick reminder of important points on your Journey.*

# *Part I*
## *The Journey Begins*

*"As you grow weary of wondering when the New Age will begin, you will decide it already did!"*

— *Lazaris*

# *One*

## *Does Anyone Really Know What The New Age Is?*

**D**oes anyone really know what the New Age is? To be sure, it is a term that is thrown around a lot. It is merrily tossed about by some Humanistic Psychologists and by certain proponents and self-proclaimed founders of the Human Potential Movement. Many who claim a certain metaphysical expertise, and others who have determined themselves as the chroniclers of reality, use the term to describe almost anything of which they approve. Detractors use the term "New Age" to describe almost anything of which they do not approve. Those who recoil from whatever the New Age is often couch their criticisms in the declaration that there is nothing "new" in the New Age. The jingle-like quality to the phrase "nothing new in the New Age" makes it sound almost true. *It is not.*

Proponents often cannot respond, not because the criticism is so profound, but rather, we would suggest, because they do not really know what this "New Age" thing they support is all about. Even those who have introduced them to the concept, especially the self-proclaimed gurus and masters, often do not know what the New Age is, either.

The term has been used so often and so universally that one presumes that everyone knows the meaning. Fearing the humiliation of ignorance, everyone nods knowingly when the term "New Age" is bandied about. We would suggest that the knowing nods only perpetuate the myths and misunderstandings.

The term "New Age" is often defined with what we have come to call the metaphysical "you-know" definition. Namely: "The New Age is . . . well, you know . . it's you know . . . well, it's kind of, you know . . . it's the age that is new, the New Age . . . you know!" To relieve the obvious discomfort, you knowingly nod and . . . Well, you know.

Does anyone really know what the New Age is? We would suggest no, most people do not know. The most lethargic re-dress the Old Age and call it new. The most energetic valiantly attempt to create whole new systems. These systems may be new, but they fall into the same old patterns of the Old Age.

To many in the Western world who have spiritual interests or yearnings, the New Age is anything Eastern. To others, it is anything novel or unusual that they do not personally know or have not personally thought of by themselves.

The definable boundaries of the New Age are so broad that you can find evidence to support this claim. There is, indeed, a good deal of Eastern metaphysics — and Western mysticism, we might add — in the whole of what is the New Age. Many of the New Age concepts of truth are both novel and seemingly unusual and unknown. New, however, means new, not old. In time, hopefully you will understand us when we say there is a great deal of new in the New Age. There is a great deal of new in the New Age!

There are many reasons for these New Age myths and misunderstandings. We would suggest that it is important to look at some of them in the attempt to figure out what the New Age really is.

## *The Old-Time Religion*

First, for some who were disenfranchised in their "old-time religion," the New Age is, we would suggest, only that same "old religion" reorganized and reworded. Their alienation stemmed from an innate and growing fear that God did not love them. God loved even the sparrow that fell, but God did not love them. They were, therefore, unlovable. Their ensuing anger and hurt produced a withdrawal from their childhood religious routine. Their guilt, however, did not change their beliefs. It just buried those beliefs. Therefore, they changed the form, but not the content, of their religion.

For the alienated, God became the "God Force" and the clerical bureaucracy became the "hierarchy." Priests and ministers became "gurus and masters." These terms, which have valid meaning on their own, became new costumes on the old figures of their childhood religion.

Coincidentally, this reorganization/rewording not only re-enfranchises the disappointed, it also puts them in charge!The anger and hurt were erroneously directed at a God they did not understand rather than at a system that did not understand them. As a result, they kept the system and threw out the God. In their reorganization they made themselves God instead of letting God be God.

Many times these alienated reorganizers are the metaphysicians who have a simple and singular answer to all issues, questions, and problems: "I am God." No matter the circumstance with which they are presented, they respond either loudly or softly with the same phrase: "I am God. You are God. He/she/it is God." They seem satisfied with this conjugation of the verb "To be God."

The pain of their disenfranchisement and their fear that God does not really love them has resulted in a denial of the existence of a God who is more than them. Initially this omnipresent statement may seem empowering. In the minds of these disenfranchised/re-enfranchised, the term eliminates a God or God Force that is more than them. We would suggest that their motivation for claiming personal Godhood is to gain leverage and ultimately advantage over a God they feel does not love them.

Think about it for a moment. If there were someone who had authority and power over you — like the old-time religion said God had — and that someone did not love you, would it not be to your strategic advantage to eliminate that someone and subsequently take their position of power? If I am God, then it does not really matter whether He loves me or not. Rather than doing something to become lovable, just eliminate the reminder that you are not!

By persuading you, they convince themselves. If they can convince you that you are already God, that you are already All That Is, then they are God, too. If they are God, then they do not have to wonder if God loves them. They do not have to worry if they are unlovable. Since they are God, they can say they love themselves, and they can say they are lovable. They can say it, but do they believe it? Do they know it?

The fear, hurt, and anger may be assuaged, but they are not resolved. The pain has blinded them to the full truth: You are a *piece* of God. The hurt has limited their awareness: *You* are God, but that *you* is bigger than the you that you now know. We would suggest that you are a piece of God and becoming, with your growth, a bigger piece.

In this situation, metaphysics becomes the old-religion with a new vocabulary. But it becomes something more: It becomes a reworded old religion filled with sublimated fear, anger, and hurt. This kind of metaphysics becomes a system of dogmatic control.

The critics become correct in this instance. There is nothing "new" in the New Age.

## *New Age but Old Form*

Owning your personal power and taking full responsibility for the reality you create — a basic New Age metaphysical concept — can be and has been squeezed into the Old Form. It can be misconstrued and misused in attempts to take power from other people rather than develop any of your own. Some are more intrigued by being in charge of other people's realities than they are with being in charge of their own. They would rather control others than be responsible for themselves. Some have used the broadness of the New Age to cloak or shroud their attempts to control.

One way it works is this: "If I hurt your feelings or caused you pain, why did YOU create that reality? Why did you create my being that way?" If the controller is on the receiving end, they respond: "You hurt me, you caused me pain. You are responsible — you did it to me. Why?"

The controller's shortcomings are your creations, and your shortcomings are your creations! They are responsible for nothing! You are responsible for all.

Another way to play this game: "Okay, I'll be responsible. YOU made me do it. If you had not done (fill in the blank), then I would not have reacted in the way I did. See, I'm being responsible. It's your fault!" The translation of this is that the controller will be responsible by blaming you. The new way of being fully responsible has been twisted and turned into the old form of blame.

A third variation is perhaps the most hurtful. Under the umbrella of the New Age, some set themselves up as the non-teacher teachers.

A non-teacher teacher is someone who ardently claims that no one is your teacher — except you. Yet you are entreated to come to their workshops and retreats to be taught, by them, that "there are no teachers."

The non-teacher teachers work with half-truths. Yes, ultimately you are your only teacher, but in the meantime there are many sources of learning. Everything in your life teaches you, and therefore is a teacher. Yet this group of teachers tells you that there are no teachers. This whole area of mental manipulation falls under the domain of these non-teacher teachers.

These non-teacher teachers lay down the non-rule rules for the new world that is to come. If you do not agree with them, it is your negative ego and just that much more evidence of your lack of enlightenment. It is a classic catch-22 reality: If you do not agree, then you are not enlightened and should not be listened to. If you have the "wisdom" or conditioning to accept everything that is said, then you are on the verge of enlightenment and deserve to be heard, but you have nothing to say!

Angered by the limitations they pretend the world has placed on them, the controllers want to create a "new" world that vindicates their trauma and validates their limitations. To fulfill the vindication and validation, they must enroll you in their "new" world.

## *Sparks of Light Barely Glowing*

The potential of the negative ego is everywhere. Within any organization or group, it can and often does exist. The negative ego aspect is a problem for the enlightened spirit and the unenlightened as well. The negative ego — whose definition uncannily parallels the definition of the Judeo-Christian Devil — can mimic metaphysical growth. Those who mimic growth by allowing their negative egos to dominate their lives fall into two groups which we call the Barely Glowing and the Dimly Lit. We would suggest that those in each group recognize the need and the desire to grow. Often their intent is pure. The problem: They give that desire and that innate need to their negative egos.

You see, the negative ego, which we personify for illustration purposes only, takes an "if-you-can't-beat-'em-join-'em" attitude when it comes to taking control of your life. More correctly, you take this attitude when you decide to run your reality from a self-important, "better-than" attitude.

The Barely Glowing and Dimly Lit groups can range from the humorously positive to the dangerously negative. In the Barely Glowing group are those who learn the rudimentary elements of the seven *chakras* today and will have a full *kundalini* rush by next Wednesday and will declare themselves fully enlightened — on the verge of ascendence — by the weekend. The Barely Glowing are the ones with a list of past lives that reads like the Who's Who of World History. These are the ones who, once they learn to meditate, are off saving the planet and the cosmos and do not have time to clean up their own lives. The Barely Glowing are too busy loving the whole human race to have time to love themselves or any ONE else.

The Barely Glowing are well-intentioned and want to love so badly — they just do not know how to direct that will or feel that love. When they are willing to let go of the negative ego, when they are willing to give up that armor, when they come out from under their bushel basket, the Barely Glowing can become the Sparks of Love that each of you intend to be.

The Dimly Lit, however, tend to delight in the "dark side." They are the ones who publicly or privately want to think they single-handedly destroyed the Lost Civilization of Atlantis. It takes an extreme arrogance to seriously believe that the negativity of one person could be that powerful. It is true that the love of one person can change the world, but love is more powerful than hate. Love is more powerful than any negative emotion. In fact, all positive emotions are more powerful than any negative emotion.

Positive emotion happens spontaneously. To feel negative, you must remember the lie. You must remember the righteousness and the blame. You must remember the self-pity and the self-importance. You must remember the illusion of the past and pretend that it's real. You must live in this illusion of physicalness and delude yourself into thinking that it is real. You must live in a world that you consciously create and pretend that it is "all happening to you." You must remember the lie.

The Dimly Lit can torment themselves as they assume the evil or dark forces are after them. These forces, the Dimly Lit whisper, are out to destroy them because (pause as they check to the left and right as the dark forces could be watching at this very moment!) they know too much. Somehow they have stumbled onto the answers that could save the world, or something like that, and the dark forces, fearing their own destruction, are out to destroy this tormented seeker.

Curious fact: These tormented ones who somehow "know too much" are strangely new to or naïve in the study of metaphysics. On the other hand, those steeped in the tradition, those who actually just might "know too much," seem to know enough to know better!

Again, it is the flattery of the negative ego that "someone knows who I am. Someone cares." It is a sad comment that some people think so little of themselves that the only caring they can conceive of as being real would be negative caring.

Another Dimly Lit approach, if not to be tormented, is to be the tormentor. They convince themselves that they can and do use demonic forces to control others. Whether you believe in demonic forces or not, people can believe and create out of that belief whatever reality they want. Maybe you do not want to believe in demonic forces, but certainly you can understand forces used demonically. This fringe group of the Dimly Lit will go so far as to decide that not only do they use the forces of the Devil, but that they are the Devil!

Fundamentalist Christians find the New Age to be covertly or overtly demonic anyway. They see the New Age as being filled with people who should be either pitied or feared, but not ignored or tolerated. The Fundamentalist Christian wants to see the New Age as some sort of monolithic force whose sole purpose is to overthrow the Christians — therefore to do the work of the Devil.

The Barely Glowing and the Dimly Lit fuel these Fundamentalists and the fundamental fears of a consensus reality. They fuel the myths and misunderstandings of the New Age. They fuel the media who love to publicize the antics of these two groups.

That there are some who profess New Age thought who neither understand what the New Age is, nor behave in an exemplary way, does not mean the whole of New Age thought is suspect — just as a backsliding Christian should not cause all of Christianity to be questioned.

## *Space Cadets and Serious Students*

Those with a strong political sense often see the New Age as the simple flights of fancy of those with overly active imaginations. We would suggest that they place the New Age, as they tend to do with so many things, on a continuum. The continuum ranges from the benign flights of fancy of "space cadets" to the dangerous indifference of social apathy of the "serious students" of metaphysics.

Indeed, there are those who cling to the New Age — again, the Dimly Lit — as a hiding place of avoidance. There are those who have drifted from one philosophical vantage point to another only to find their "loser" reality repeated over and over again. As they drift into an arena called the "New Age," they can and often do get lost in their flights of fancy. Some do become "space cadets" of the New Age, that is true. Others, we would suggest, after resting awhile in the safety of their illusions, do wake up and a light goes on, so to speak. We would suggest that many heal themselves while wandering around in their fantasies. They wake up — that is, a light goes on in the mind and heart of the Dimly Lit — and they become "enlightened," and either move out of their fantasies into a more productive expression of their spirituality, or they stay in their fantasies and manifest them into reality. The "space cadet" graduates into the "innovative genius."

Everyone manifests their Dreams — but not necessarily their fantasies. We define a Dream as the adult synergy of desire, imagination, and expectancy. When you combine these various ingredients, a whole is created that is more — oh, so very much more! — than just the sum of the parts. A Dream is born, a Dream that also has a sub-text of maximizing who you are, and a super-text of becoming more than you are.

A fantasy, on the other hand, is an adolescent adventure in imagination without any real desire and no solidly determined expectation. The words may be there with great drama and even greater bravado, but the "guts" are missing. In fact, a characteristic of a fantasy is that the potential manifestation is seen as a threat and as a source of fear rather than as something to celebrate and a source of joy.

A "space cadet" is either someone who is hiding in their adolescent fantasy, which they never really want to have manifest, or is someone who is dreaming a dream that no one understands yet.

Certainly Albert Einstein was considered a "cadet." In fact, Einstein had a dream one night. He dreamed about what it would be like to ride on a beam of light. He was so taken with this dream that he could not let it go. He was a "cadet" with a dream that no one could even begin to understand. He was a "cadet" until that dream evolved and manifested into the Theories of Relativity.

Closer to home, a dear friend who lives in Texas learned about working on the Causal Plane of reality with our 33-second technique. She decided to create a car, but not just any car. She had a make and style very clearly in mind. She knew the color and all the luxury extras she wanted. The price of her dream was much more than her budget could allow. Even monthly payments for an expensive sports car were out of the question. To have what she wanted would require having a dream come true!

She let everyone know she was going to create this reality by using our techniques. Those who could not understand her dream dismissed her compassionately as a "space cadet." Others who were threatened by her dream dismissed her more cruelly as a fool.

Within a week she met a man. It is not what you think! He was in a financial bind and needed help. He had a car. He had to sell it. Yes, it was the exact car she had created in her mind -- it was her dream. How could she afford it?

He asked her to help him out by purchasing the car for payments — no money down — just take over the payments. She *could* believe it! This was a dream, not a fantasy! The payments were not several hundred dollars per month, as many might suspect. The payments were only $125.00 per month!

When she drove her dream, she was no longer a "space cadet" or a fool. People began asking her to "just dream a little dream for me."

We would suggest that when the "space cadet" who is dreaming the dream manifests it, the scoffs turn to cheers as they graduate from "space cadet" to "innovative genius." Their past is quickly forgotten by everyone else. They remember.

The "cadet" who is hiding from the world by getting lost in a fantasy is a product of the world, not of the New Age. Despite what the critics and detractors say, these "cadets" have been a part of your world and of your society since the beginning. The New Age has given them a chance to breathe — has given them a chance to either turn the fantasies into dream and then manifest them, or to create a safe world from which they no longer feel a need to hide. With safety, they can let go of the fantasy.

Certain of the myths and misunderstandings about the New Age have, perhaps, encouraged those "close to the edge" to become "space cadets" — perhaps they would have anyway. However, the New Age has also offered some of the "cadets" a way back from their fantasies into a functional and productive world.

What about the "serious student" who is criticized for apathy or decadence? It is sadly true that there are some who consider themselves "serious students" who have a shallow understanding of creating their own reality. They often are apathetic. They adopt reality creation as merely a convenient philosophy to avoid being responsible for their world, rather than as a truth with which to responsibly change their world.

Those who fit into this category should perhaps be called "shallow students," not "serious students." There are also some who use metaphysics and the panoply of the New Age as armor against responsibility. We would suggest that these are the ones who find responsibility frightening. Therefore, they twist the basic tenets of reality creation to justify non-participation in and non-caring for the world in which they — and you — live.

The indifference of the "shallow student" can be dangerous. They do not participate in the world because their shallow understanding leads them to say only that whoever is suffering is creating that suffering. True, so far. Therefore, they say, it has nothing to do with them. Untrue. These "shallow students" conveniently forget that they also are creating the reality. Though they are not the ones suffering, they are the ones aware of the suffering they cavalierly dismiss as "not their problem."

If you are aware of the problem, you are a part of it. We will say that again: If you are aware of the problem, you are a part of it.

The actual serious student who has an in-depth understanding of reality creation knows this. The true student of metaphysics sees the awareness of a problem as an opportunity to participate in the solution, not as just another opportunity to blame and absolve themselves of participation.

The socially conscious critics are correct when they see a danger in the New Age when they are dealing with the shallow student. Those same critics are incorrect when they lump the true serious students in with the shallow ones.

We would suggest that the indifference of the shallow student is not a product of the New Age. Their indifference is a product of fear and impotence. If the New Age were not available to them, they would find another place to hide.

## *Who Really Suffers?*

The limited definitions and the overly simple criticisms are allowed to stand, we would suggest, because very few even know what the "New Age" is. Further, the principles of non-judgment are ambiguously understood and are often incorrectly taught in the New Age milieu, so no one objects to the erroneous descriptions and criticisms for fear of appearing judgmental.

We would suggest that it is not important to convince the detractors, that is true. The detractors are always going to find fault, because their condemnation is really their fear in disguise. To eliminate their criticism is only to remove their mask, not to answer their fear. They will just find a new mask behind which to hide — they will just find a new criticism or a new rationale to justify their condemnation. No, we would suggest, it is not important to respond to their criticism or to convince the unbelieving detractor. We would suggest that eventually it will be important to respond to the fear, but not to the criticism.

It is the proponent of the New Age — whatever that term means — who suffers when the erroneous definitions and the bogus criticisms are allowed to stand, are allowed to go unanswered. The true seekers can become discouraged, can be misguided, in their search. Indeed, some may even leave their journey behind because of being entangled in a web of misunderstanding.

An interesting human phenomenon: When you get completely caught in a web of misunderstanding, you think there is no exit from your imprisonment. You are impotent. You are scared. You are angry. If you can entice others to be similarly trapped, however, you think you become free. The more people you can entangle in your limitations, the freer you think you will become. Out of fear and anger, you do not seek understanding and solution, you seek people — as many people as possible — to ensnare or enslave in your own now-institutionalized misunderstanding. The ploy, we would suggest, does not work. Rather than aborting this misguided attempt at freedom, you insatiably seek more people to ensnare or enslave. You seek more participants to entangle.

No, the critic is not consciously hurt by the myths and misunderstandings: The critic is fueled by them. The shallow students and the bandwagoneers — those who have hopped on the bandwagon of growth and the New Age — are not hurt: They have other agendas than growth. You are hurt, you, the true seeker who is stretching and reaching in search of a journey, a special journey Home, a Sacred Journey back to God/Goddess/All That Is.

## *Personal Responsibility*

Does anyone really know what the New Age is? Yes. *The New Age is an Age of Humanity, an Age of Consciousness, in which each individual willingly and enthusiastically accepts personal responsibility for consciously creating reality.* Willingness, we would suggest, is an important part of this responsible reality creation.

We would suggest that the Old Age was filled with obligatory responsibility which quickly becomes a grand source of struggle, sacrifice, and suffering. The obligatory responsibility connotes blame and its ensuing punishment.

Too often, when you hear the word "responsibility," your mind races back to a time in your childhood, and you hear your mother's voice both sweetly and menacingly asking, "Who is responsible for this mess?" You were told to admit it now — it (the necessary punishment) would be easier if you did. Always the words responsibility and wrong-doing were associated, if not synonymous. No one ever came into your perfectly spotless bedroom and asked who was responsible for the neatness! Such positive incidents were met with such phrases as, "It's about time," or "Well, there's hope for you yet!"

Now when you even hear the word your inner child retreats, and you run the other way. What could honestly be the "fun" of responsibility seems like anything but fun. The opportunity of responsibility becomes the resentment and bitterness of responsibility.

This admonishing responsibility is also an integral part of the consensus reality along with the guilt of failing to be responsible. We would suggest that this kind of so-called responsibility is not a part of the New Age. If you define responsibility in these terms, indeed, there is nothing new here.

Responsibility: The ability to respond. Please indulge a rather silly analogy — silly, but effective. Suppose your telephone begins to ring. Sitting across the room, you say hello. Nothing happens. You say hello again. No one responds. You try again only much louder this time. Still nothing. Why? Obviously, you did not pick up the receiver. To be able to respond, you must go to the telephone, pick up the receiver, place the mouthpiece within some proximity of your mouth and then say hello.

What can keep you from responding? What can keep you from taking the necessary steps ultimately to engage in a conversation?   Well, we would suggest that any number of things, including physical, emotional, and mental limitations (being unable to walk or to hear, a mechanical malfunction perhaps, fear of people or of the unknown, or projections of unpleasant news) can prevent you from responding. Additionally, some may have psychic or intuition limitations — intuitive forebodings.

If you are unable to respond to a situation, we would suggest, you are not being responsible. In your real life, there are many things that "keep" you from responding to things which are much more important than your telephone.

Inertia (being stuck in habituated patterns of behavior) and psychological projection/identification are the most common. We would suggest that in a world that is constantly expanding and changing, inertia results in a downward spiral of ineffectiveness. Because you will not think or feel, and therefore will not take action, you are unable to respond to the current reality. You end up waiting for someone or something to make your life work. You end up standing still in a world that is ever moving forward. If you are not moving with that world (or faster), you are falling backwards.

When you project (usually parent) onto other people, you automatically identify yourself (usually as child). If, as a man, you act and react to a woman as though she were your mother, you have placed yourself as child by default. When she seems unhappy you wonder what you did wrong — like a boy would — rather than wondering if she is all right — like a man might wonder.

When you project child you must always identify, correspondingly, as parent. When a person is afraid of other people's power, they often react by seeing those other people as children. Many men want to see the woman in their life as a cute little girl because the "woman" she is frightens them. Also, many women want to think of their men as just little boys in big bodies because the "man" that otherwise just might be there scares them. When you want to see another grown-up as a mere child, you will make yourself the parent — usually the authoritative or judgmental parent — usually behaving just like your parents behaved!

For others, projection is a side effect of their desire to identify. If you see yourself as the "nice guy," then you must project "not-so-nice guy" onto others. If you identify yourself as the smartest person you know, then you must project ignorance onto those around you. When you identify yourself as the strongest one, the one everyone leans on, then you will surround yourself with weak people, and you will project that weakness, if necessary.

When you project/identify, you are not being the adult in the present time/space reality. You are therefore not able to respond any more effectively than the person sitting across the room screaming "hello" at that ringing telephone.

Boredom, vengeful jealousy, and guilt, worry, or depression are also inhibitors of responsible action. Boredom is the higher octave of inertia. When you refuse to think and feel, when you refuse to act, you get bored. Eventually you will stagnate in your own boredom, unable and unwilling to respond to your world. "Too bored to stay in bed — too bored not to."

When the projections do not work — when that woman will not cooperate and be your mother, when the boss just will not become your father — you can turn bitter. Jealousy and revenge are the higher and more hostile octaves of projection.

Though you try to hold the "identification" in place, you slip, it slips, something happens. You feel guilt, worry, or depression. These three combine to create the higher octave of identification and you stop actively taking responsibility.

All these qualities lead to the ultimate rationale for denying or refusing responsible reality creation: Self-pity. Be it victimhood, martyrhood, or self-pity *au naturel*, self-pity is the bottom line of responsibility abnegation.

The right to be a victim and the right to be victimized are cornerstones of that which is the Old Age. We would suggest, the right quickly becomes a necessity in the current consensus reality.

The New Age, unlike the detractors accuse, does not really claim there is no such thing as victimhood or victims. We would suggest, the New Age is an Age of Humanity where people strive to replace the very real feeling of self-pity with the much more exciting and reliable feelings of enthusiasm and love.

We know that some in the field of metaphysics categorically state that there is no such thing as a victim. This is crazy-making, over-simplified metaphysics which both encourages and fuels the critics, and discourages and distances the real seeker.

You hear that there is no such thing as a victim, and then you look around you and your world, and, like it or not, we would suggest, there are victims —

THE SACRED JOURNEY 14

those who have created their reality without full conscious awareness, without conscious responsibility. Yes, they have created their own reality, and therefore they must have wanted it that way. However, until they know that and then consciously choose that, they are victims — self-created victims, but victims nonetheless.

When a person realizes that they do indeed create their own reality and that they do it consciously, then they have a choice. Then they can stop being a victim, or they can continue. It is their choice. Once it is their choice, then we would agree with the chorus: "There are no victims."

We would suggest that if that person persists in being a victim once they know they have a choice, they are doing so as a manipulative ploy. They are no longer a victim; they are a manipulator.

There are victims in your world. In the New Age there is an opportunity to end victimhood and martyrhood altogether. That ending, however, is not going to happen by eliminating the word from your vocabulary!

## *Conscious Creation*

The other significant key to understanding this concept of the New Age is understanding "consciously creating your reality." Humanistic and other leading-edge psychologies, as well as contemporary religions, agree that each person creates their reality. That is, they will agree that you create your own reality by your attitude. If you are feeling paranoid, it will seem like everyone is out to get you, and you may create a miserable reality as a result. Your attitude may cause you to act hastily; it may cause you to do foolish things, and thus you created your own reality. If, on the other hand, you are expecting life to be great, the mishaps will be ignored. Notice, the suggestion is that the mishaps will still occur — it's just that you will not notice or care.

Among the proponents of conscious reality creation, few will go so far as to say you create your own reality literally. They may say your attitude will affect the way you view the "things" of your life, but they will not say that your attitude will literally create those very "things!"

We would suggest: Many who claim metaphysical expertise are capable of pronouncing the words, but based on the disclaimers and limiters that they place on this concept, based on the exceptions they list, it is obvious that they do not really believe that they do create their own reality. Certainly they act as though they do not want you to believe it!

You do create it all. There are no exceptions. There is no fine print.

There are no asterisks. Not only do you create the way you look at things, you create the very things you look at!

That statement could be repeated unendingly. Not only do you create the way you look at things, you create the very things you look at! You create all of your reality, and you do it consciously.

The quantum physicists in your reality are demonstrating more than ever the truth of that statement. The only theories and paradigms of reality that consistently work are based on several common themes: Reality is an illusion created by observation and/or by consciousness. Reality, at best, is a probability created out of thought. Reality is an illusion of light trapped by observation and thought.

It is always curious to us that a scientific-type person will often scoff at the conscious creation concept and, at the same time, they will enthusiastically support the "double-blind" procedure in scientific experimentation. We would suggest that the double-blind procedure was developed as a response to the quantum understanding that *there is no such thing as an observer.* Everyone is a participant in creating the results of an experiment. In other words, the expectations of the investigator have impact upon the results. Thought in the form of expectation has impact — is a determining factor — in the reality created in the experimental laboratory. If the experimenter expects a certain food to produce cancer in rats, it most likely will — perhaps because of the food, but definitely because of the experimenter's thought! The scientific type has difficulty accepting this concept of conscious creation. Actually, it is more difficult to accept the idea that thought has so much impact inside the scientific laboratory and so little impact outside the laboratory! How does thought know where it is?

Whereas the Old Age has many interpretive meanings for the concept of reality creation, the New Age is quite clear: You consciously create your own reality either by causing it or by allowing it.

## Reality = *Self-Generated Illusion*

*The New Age is an Age of Humanity — an Age of Consciousness — in which each individual personally and practically comprehends that their world is a self-generated illusion that is limited only by their unique choices and decisions, their private thoughts and feelings, and their personal attitudes and beliefs.* + expectations

That reality is a self-generated illusion is the greatest liberating concept in your world today. As with any liberating concept, many fear it and attack it with a vengeance.  Reflect for a moment on your political history where several liberating concepts have been born.  From the initial concepts of truths held self-evident in your Constitution to the liberating ideas of feminism, each of these concepts, we would suggest, was feared and attacked as dangerous and detrimental to the moral fiber of life.

Critics of the conscious creation concept often attack with the question, "How do you tell a starving person anywhere in the world, or how do you tell a rape victim, that they create their own reality — that they created starving or being raped?"  The critics huff that such behavior would be more than insensitive. It would be cruel.

The naïve proponent, in their zeal to defend metaphysics and the New Age, is drawn into this line of criticism by defending this hypothetical behavior which, indeed, would be both insensitive and cruel.

We would suggest that the true metaphysician would not tell a starving person or a rape victim anything about reality creation — at first. Initially, they would work to heal the wound.  Then, once whole again, they would talk of things metaphysical.

A major criticism of American Foreign Policy in the late '50's and early '60's was that the American policymaker did not understand that you cannot talk to the politically oppressed and physically starving about the Bill of Rights and the genius of Jefferson.  First you must do something about their food situation, then talk of loftier things.  Fill their bellies and then their minds.

In the '50's and '60's, should the American political system have been abandoned as cruel and insensitive, and therefore wrong, because of a misapplication of its principles?  Certainly not.  Then why should the whole of metaphysics and the New Age be so abandoned because of a hypothetical misapplication of principle?

The critic and the true proponent would heal the wound first.  They would deal with the emotion and the emotional scars.  We would suggest that once the victim was well, each would proceed differently.  The metaphysician would offer hope for a different future by talking of conscious reality creation. The critic would offer hope by encouraging political and economic reform that will hopefully come sometime in the future when the proper political leadership can be established etc., etc., etc.  In fact, which approach is more compassionate?

Admittedly, we do not have a body.  However, if we did and that body were violated, in time we would want to know that we created that reality, because then we could do something about it in the future.  Knowing that we either caused it or allowed it is a grand source of power — liberating power. To convince ourselves that we are hopelessly a victim and that there is nothing we can do to prevent the nightmare from occurring again — to convince ourselves that we have to wait and hope that others, i.e. political policymakers and governmental bureaucrats, will do something to make us safe — is frightening at best.

First you heal the wound, whether it is a physical, mental, emotional, or psychic wound. You heal it first. Then you recognize, acknowledge, forgive yourself and others, if appropriate, and change the reality by comprehending that you indeed do create it all.

## Boundaries of Creation

There are limits to what you can self-generate. The initial limits are your unique choices and decisions. Every day you make choices and, out of those choices, you make decisions as to how your life is going to work. From the moment you wake up, you are silently choosing to be happy or sad, pleased or disappointed, content or angry. We would suggest: You are often not aware of such choices because you have habituated them into automatic decisions. There are people (certainly you've seen them) who have decided to be miserable. No matter what happens or what is said, they are determined to be unhappy. They not only generate an attitude, they put out a field of energy — an almost magnetic field — that literally attracts miserable things happening in their reality. From every traffic light being red to everyone giving them more "bad news" about their reality, they create it all according to the choices, and the decisions that grow out of those basic choices. As you can see it in them, so you can discover it in yourself. That it is automatic does not make it less powerful.

The next limits are the thoughts you think and the feelings you feel. Finally, we would suggest that attitudes and beliefs conclude the limits on the reality you can create. The most powerful of the limiters? Your beliefs.

As these components are limiters, we would also suggest that they are the raw materials out of which the illusion is made. As they provide the boundary of what is possible, they also stretch the very boundaries they create. As these raw materials provide the limits, they also provide the liberation!

As you make new choices and decisions, as you wake up and consciously choose, and then from those new choices decide to be happy and to have a successful day, so you will. As you slow down long enough to listen to the thoughts and feelings you have, and more importantly, we would suggest, as you change your thoughts and feelings, as you change them consciously, so you more consciously create your own reality. Similarly, as you monitor your attitudes and your beliefs, as you make the choice to hold more positive attitudes and more inspirational beliefs, so your reality becomes more positive and inspiring.

## *The Power of Belief*

One of the most difficult metaphysical concepts: *Belief creates experience.* The consensus reality, we would suggest, teaches that experience comes first, and that out of those experiences, belief is somehow born. The domination of Newtonian science — which says that all proof is based on repeatable experience — has had a profound influence on the way you see your world. The sciences of the quantum, however, categorically prove that Newton, though well-intentioned, was wrong!

The quantum suggests that reality is created not out of experience, but out of expectation. Reality is a product of what you expect to experience, which is another way of saying: Belief creates experience.

Belief creates experience. Choice manifests it.

## *Personal Power without Loneliness*

*The New Age is an Age of Humanity — an Age of Consciousness — in which each individual joyously takes back their personal power and becomes their own master-creator in a co-creating relationship with God/Goddess/All That Is.*

We would suggest, perhaps, that enough has been said about the dangers of giving your power to other people and about the importance of taking your power back from those sincere and insincere gurus and masters. Even the naïve are aware of the efficacy of this attitude, even if they do not adhere to it.

Two points, we would suggest, are often overlooked. First, many will tell you to watch out for the people who want to take your power. They are right. There are many who are in the "business" of growth for the very purpose of trying to take your power. Sometimes they seek your power because they do not believe they have any of their own, or their own isn't enough or "good enough." Sometimes, we would suggest, they seek your power just to see if they can get it — just for the "fun" of it. They prey upon your eagerness to grow. They prey upon your hungry heart. There is no excuse or justification for such behavior. Buyer beware!

What about the power you give away and are encouraged to give away to the real enslavers? What about the power you give to the Past in your continued attempts to re-live it — in your continued attempts to fix it or make it right? What about the power you give to the Future? How much of your power is given to waiting for future vindication of past injustice? How much of Now is lost while you hold your breath waiting for someone else to make the future all right? How much energy do you throw away fearing what the future may hold? When are you going to take your power back from the enslavement of the Past and Future?

What about the enslavement of the Present that the consensus reality locks up in a maze of inevitabilities? What about the power lost in the "fact" and "logic" of an ever-oppressive present? The Past, Future, and Present, we would suggest, can be grand and glorious tools of growth, or each of them can be an enslaver. You must decide to take back your power — not only from the human gurus and masters, but also from the "gurus and masters" you have made of the Past, Future, and Present.

Time and Space were created by you to assist you in your learning experience of the physical. Then you gave your power away to Time and to Space. You allowed them, we would suggest, to dictate your reality to you. How much of who you are, of what you do, and of what you think — how much of your identity — is controlled by Time and Space? How much of your desire and expectancy is dictated by the time you think you have and by the space you feel is available? How much of your imagination is harnessed by the shacklers of Time and Space? We would suggest that you have given the power of dreaming to the master *née* servant of Time and Space.

Yes, it is important to take back power from any source to whom you have given it. It is also important to be aware of where you have given away — where you have lost — your power.

Secondly, in the New Age people take back their power in a co-creating relationship with God/Goddess/All That Is, not alone. They become their own master-creator in a co-creating relationship with God/Goddess/All That Is, not alone. When it comes to taking back your power, so often you speak the proper words, but ignore the corresponding action, because you are afraid of loneliness.

The grandest fear and the original fear: The fear of loneliness. To be either encouraged or admonished to take back your power and to become your own master-creator is a scary proposition if you must do it alone.

You are not stupid metaphysical low-life just because you will not take back your power — like you have been told to do. You are scared. You are scared of being all alone and thus lonely. Your mythology tells you that taking any kind of power is a dangerous proposition. Prometheus took fire.

According to your legends, Fire was the symbol of power held by the gods, and when Prometheus took it, the gods feared that the real power — immortality — would be taken next. In the Judeo-Christian mythology, we would suggest, Eve and then Adam took back their power. The knowledge of good and evil — the ability to choose and to discern — is power. God feared that the real power — immortality — would be next. God, according to the story, cast them out, and you have been trying to "get back in" ever since. Taking back your power has some serious ramifications, according to your mythology, namely, that you will be rejected and cast into a state of separation and loneliness.

Taking back your power in the Old Age is still a frightening proposition. Mythology notwithstanding, there are parental, educational, and religious pressures "telling" you not to be powerful.

These pressures, though intense, are expected, and you are able to compensate for them. Often unexpected is the additional pressure from an Old Age that mimics the New that similarly discourages re-capturing the power that you have overtly and covertly given away.

When you willingly become powerful in relationship with God/Goddess/All That Is and willingly become your own master-creator with God/Goddess/All That Is, there is no aloneness/loneliness. Instead, there is a celebratory freedom!

## A World of Dominion

**The New Age is an Age of Humanity — an Age of Consciousness — in which each individual lovingly and celebratorily creates a world of Dominion rather than one of Domination.**

A World of Domination, we would suggest, can be characterized in the following way. It is a world where you must:

1.   Manipulate or be manipulated, control or be controlled.

2.   See power as the ability to rule over people, as the ability to overpower.

3.   Accept your wretchedness, calling for God to pity you as you pity yourself. To get God's love, you believe, you must manipulate for it.

4.   Continuously relive the Past attempting to do it right — to make it

perfect — and continuously support the negative ego and its desire to be "better than" everyone else.

5.   Live in a world that is unfair — live in a world that is globally and personally unfriendly.

6.   Take or be taken.

7.   Blame or be blamed.


The Old Age is an age of Domination. Do not confuse domination with a political dictatorship. Dictatorship is oppressive domination, but domination is not necessarily dictatorial. Domination often shows itself as weakness. The dominating person can be a bully, but is much more often the victim. When a bully finds a victim, the victim, we would suggest, is the one in control. Consider this: In a relationship between a bully and a victim, when the bully stops being a bully, the victim can still be a victim. However, when the victim stops, the bully must stop, too. Bullies need victims. Victims do not "need" anyone.

Belief creates experience. If you believe "that's the way the world is," then naturally that is the way of the world — for you. However, more than belief is at work here. The belief colors the attitude which, in turn, influences the thoughts and feelings about the consensus reality of domination. Additionally, the decisions you make about how to function in a dominating world have impact on the your daily choices.

Your daily choices to dominate then germinate into dominating decisions. We would suggest that these decisions sprout into thoughts and feelings which in turn blossom into attitudes and beliefs of domination. The system becomes self-perpetuating. No new input about a dominating world is necessary. You have created your own little "eco-system" of misinformation.

## *There are Fractions*

In mathematics, there is a theory called The Set Theory. Simply put, it says that if you are inside a Set, you cannot be outside of that Set. That may seem so simple that it has dipped below the level of understanding. Let us try again. In a Set of All Whole Numbers, there are no fractions. As soon as there is even one fraction, it is no longer a Set of All Whole Numbers.

The theory also says that you cannot fully understand a Set until you are outside of it. That is, you cannot fully understand that The Set of All Whole Numbers is, in fact, a Set made up of all whole numbers until you have discovered a Set that has more than just whole numbers.  While you are inside The Set of All Whole Numbers, you may think that it is all the numbers that are possible in the world.  Therefore, you think, "this set stuff is a bunch of nonsense!"

More sophisticatedly, you may think the whole numbers in your Set are indeed in a Set, but that the Set is a Set of All Numbers (whole or otherwise) — that the Set you are in is the only Set available — that the Set you are in should be called The Set of All Numbers not The Set of All **Whole** Numbers.

Once you discover fractions . . . Oh my, how your world changes!

Many of you and much of your world, we would suggest, belong to a set called **WORLD**.  That is, you and your world call it **WORLD** just as some want to call a Set of All Whole Numbers simply a Set of All Numbers.  It more appropriately should be called **WORLD OF DOMINATION** (rather than just **WORLD**).  This is a more proper label or set name because there is another Set — there is another world.  There is a Set called **WORLD OF DOMINION!**

The critics and detractors are stuck in a world of domination that they call the only world there is.  In their stagnation of limitation and fear, they laugh at you for even "wondering if."  They criticize you for the heresy of admitting that maybe (and they attack you if you realize) you are in a Set.  There are other Sets.  You are in a world.  There are other worlds.  There is a World of Dominion.

The World of Dominion is a world in which you may:

1.  Creatively generate your reality without falling back on manipulation or control.

2.  Know power is the ability to act and the willingness to act, not requiring "power over" to be effective.

3.  Approach God/Goddess/All That Is as partner to co-create your reality.  You may ask for help, not pity.  You may have a non-manipulative relationship with God/Goddess/All That Is.

4.  Continuously reach and stretch for your future reality and allow it to be more — allow it to be more loving.  Continuously support your Future Self and your Spiritual Self.

5.  Live in a world that initially is personally friendly and then is globally friendly.  Experience the world as your support system and ally.

6.  Give.

7. Love.

The New Age is about recognizing which Set you are in. It is about stepping out of the Old Set, the Old Age and Old World, into the New Set — The New Age and New World.

## *It Is Real*

Does anyone really know what the New Age is? Yes. It is an Age when people willingly and joyously accept personal responsibility for the world they are in and have created. Then they begin a powerful personal journey, using choice and decision, thought and feeling, and attitude and belief as the raw materials of change. They sculpt and carve and chisel their reality with desire, expectation, and imagination. They create their own reality out of Dreams and Visions. They both consciously create and co-create with God/Goddess/All That Is a new world of Dominion. They create and co-create a new dawn, a new day, a New Age of Humanity. It is real. It is real.

The mystics of your ancient past, we would suggest, knew it was real. The soothsayers and prophets knew it was real, too. Recorded prophecy, prolific through the ages, comes abruptly to a stop at the end of the 20th Century and at the beginning of the 21st. Many point with a quaking finger claiming that this is proof of an End that is near. Yes. Yes, we would suggest that an end is near: An End to the Old Age and the beginning of a New Age.

Those who were insightful enough to be so profound in their predictions were, similarly, insightful enough to know not to make predictions for an Age of Humanity when people take their power back and proceed first to consciously create their own personal reality, and then to consciously create their own global reality, out of and with their individual relationship with God/Goddess/All That Is.

You see, in the Old Age you created your own reality, but you were not willing to be conscious of it. Therefore, we would suggest that the blueprint of the future that you laid out in your subconscious mind was the blueprint you lived out consciously. Those who were sensitive enough to see or read your subconscious blueprint could foretell your conscious future with astounding accuracy. When an individual steps into the New Age, however, reality is created consciously, and therefore the blueprint of the future can be changed at will — at your Free Will. Those who are sensitive enough to *honestly* see or read your blueprint are also humble enough to speak no longer of absolute futures, but instead they speak of possible and probable futures. The operative word here is "honestly."

As you step into the New Age, the futures become your futures. They become what you want them to be. As more and more of you step into it, the New Age becomes more real than the Old. Then the soothsayers stop saying. The prophets stop prophesying.

## *When Does the New Age Begin?*

The Christians speak of the time of Revelation. Many argue a specific date in the illusion of time. The Bible reports, we would suggest, that when Jesus was asked about the Second Coming, he told the woman questioning him not to get pregnant, for he would return before she could give birth. Admittedly, we have not been physical, but by our calculations, the Second Coming would occur within nine months! Something is amiss!

The enlightened Christian now knows that the Book of Revelations is depicting a symbolic Second Coming of the Christ Consciousness. The First Coming was reported in the Bible; the Second Coming is a personal Revelation of the Christ Consciousness within. Even traditional Christians, we would suggest, are beginning to understand the private nature of a new and renewed relationship with their Prince of Peace and Son of God. Fundamentalist Christians still hold out for a specific date.

The New Age, similarly, is a personal experience. Do not wait for a specific astrological day and date. Do not wait for others to tell you when to begin. "I will take back my power as soon as you give me permission" is a contradictory and stagnating statement. Fundamentalist metaphysicians still want to calculate and arbitrate a very specific date. Traditional metaphysicians are willing to consider that maybe, just maybe, the New Age begins with some sort of critical mass. They wander around mumbling something about 99 monkeys or something like that.

Critical Mass and the 99th Monkey Theory suggest that when a certain magical number of people become enlightened, that when a certain magical number of people enter the New Age, everyone will be enlightened and everyone will be in the New Age. Though these theories are appealing to some — particularly to those who do not want to be responsible for or conscious of the reality they create — neither theory, we would suggest, is correct.

For years many have been pointing to this 99th Monkey theory as scientific proof of Critical Mass. Upon scrutiny of the scientific data cited, however, we would suggest that one becomes embarrassingly aware that no such proof exists. The evidence cited suggested that after a certain number of monkeys learned to wash potatoes before eating them, the number of potato-washing monkeys grew exponentially. What the advocates of critical mass left out was that the potato-washing monkeys were all pregnant monkeys who all gave birth at approximately the same time! The births, we would suggest, accounted for the exponential increase in potato-washing, not critical mass. What was proved in the 99th Monkey Theory was that mothers teach their young, not that there is "critical mass."

Throughout the history of humankind, people have been seeking. Many have found. In the midst of your Old Age, others have discovered their New Age. It happens for each person individually. Don't wait!

The enlightened metaphysician "remembers" that the New Age begins when they, individually, step with elegance out of the Old World into the New. It begins with one and then another and then one more. As more and more people seek and find, we would suggest, it makes it easier for even more to similarly reach and stretch.

Each of you must do it for yourself, but, as more of you decide to grow, it becomes easier and easier to do it for yourself. The Universe is in perfect harmony. Now, when so many are so quick to tell you how terrible your world has become, is the easiest time of all to step into the New Dawn, the New Day, the New World, the New Age!

Does anyone really know what the New Age Is? Take a step. Find out for yourself. Let the journey begin.

# *Part II*
## *The Four Choices To Grow*

*"The search is on:   Who founded the Human Potential Movement?   The potential to be human began with the feeling **There is more to life than just surviving . . . there must be more**.   Who felt that feeling first?   You did!"*

— *Lazaris*

# TWO

## *The Four Choices To Grow*

The New Age is a personal process of discovery. Each person enters their own New Age when they are willing. Amidst your Old Age, someone has discovered their New Age. How did it all begin?

When you were one with God/Goddess/All That Is, you were a spark of consciousness, an unidentifiable spark of light, a piece of Love who did not know ... You were a piece of Love who did not know.

At a time before Time, in a space before Space, that boundary-less Love desired. It desired to know itself. In its desire to know, Love expected. It expected to find an answer, though it knew not what that answer would be. In its desire and expectancy, Love imagined. Love wondered, "Why ... ?"

Why what? You cannot know the answer to that question because that Love, that boundary-less Love which is God/Goddess/All That Is, has not yet finished asking it. The thought is not yet complete.

All that has transpired in all the illusions in all your realities from the beginning of time to the present has occurred in the catch of a breath of Love. When you are once again at one with God/Goddess/All That Is, the question will be complete, the answer known.

It all begins and continues as Love dreams, as God/Goddess/All That Is dreams. Love that is God/Goddess/All That Is dreams of its own existence and wonders why.  As the process of wondering why occurs in the macrocosmic sense, so, we would suggest, it occurs in the microcosm of your life and concurrent lives.  You too wonder:  Why?  When you do, your growth begins.

With the initial and continuing explosion of the question, the one spark becomes many.  The many, similarly, put the question and explode.  The many become the many more.  The many more put the question . . .  After many more, there is a spark of consciousness — there is a you — that is called your Higher Self.  There is a piece of Love who wants to grow.

When you decide to begin to grow in the physical form, we would suggest, you do not just pop into a sophisticated human form filled with Spiritual awakening.  You could, but you do not.  The main reason you do not is because on a very deep level you know that the key to growth is not found in the ends of a process, but in the means.

For example, a dear friend of ours is a rather special artist.  Though he enjoys looking at the finished product of his creativity, a greater joy comes from the actual brush-stroke-by-brush-stroke process of painting it in the first place.  Often he will forget what he has already completed, preferring the expectation of what he will be painting.  But nothing is as wondrous for him as getting lost and then found anew in what he is currently painting.  The joy and the learning is in the means, not the end.

The end of growth:  Becoming one with God/Goddess/All That Is.  The end is guaranteed.  You will eventually accomplish this end result.  The growth is the process of getting there.  The growth is the difficulty or ease — the clumsiness or elegance — with which you achieve the end.

You see, you are a piece of the Source.  You cannot lose that.  You can pretend you are separate, but you can never be separate.  Enlightenment is about ending the pretense.  When you stop pretending you will realize what has been true all along:  You are one with the Source — you are one with The Love.

The end, becoming one with The Source, will happen.  The means to accomplish that end, we would suggest, are what really matter.  Do not concern yourself with whether you are going to grow, or if you are going to "make it."  Instead, we would suggest, turn your attention to *how* you are going to grow, and when.

The initial choice is to grow.  However, you do not just pop into humanness with a fully developed potential.  You begin with an initial choice and make many more "initial choices" along the way.

## The Initial Kingdoms

With the explosion of consciousness and the decision to grow, one of the first questions is: Do you want to grow in a dense form (physically) or in a light form (non-physically)?  Once you have decided to grow in a dense world, there are a series of questions you ask yourself which lead to choosing the particular universe, galaxy, solar system and planet in which to do that growing.  Your initial explorations into the density were cautious and delicate. You began as thought energy, raw thought, but thought energy nonetheless. Then you became denser and expressed yourself as consciousness units of thought, undefined but willing consciousness units of thought.  Then you manifested yourself as sub-atomic and then atomic particles.

Thought has its own desire to grow.  Consciousness units — thoughts working in synergy — have expectations.  Sub-atomic and atomic particles dream of being atoms and yearn to accomplish more.  They dream of becoming more of who they are.  As the next step in their growth atoms reach for The Mineral Kingdom.

There is no reincarnation in the Mineral Kingdom.  You do not enter as a piece of gravel and evolve into a precious diamond or anything.  No.  You experience the Mineral Kingdom for whatever length of time you feel is necessary.  Some of you will spend relatively little time here because, for reasons that are your own, it is not necessary to your Journey Home.  Others, we would suggest, will spend a great deal of time in this Kingdom.  Whatever is right for you will automatically happen on this level of the physical and at this level of consciousness.  When you are "done" — when you have experienced what you need to experience — you will move to the next kingdom.

The Plant Kingdom offers a different level of learning.  Similarly, there is no concept of reincarnation in this Kingdom, either.  You do not begin as a dusty roadside weed with visions of someday being an orchid or whatever. No.  Once again, you will decide what it is that you need to learn, and you will do it in the most elegant way possible.  Some, we would suggest, may choose to be a day lily.  Others of you may select to express yourself as a sequoia.  It all depends on what you decide you need to know.

## The Dream of the Devas

In each of these Kingdoms, you learn what you feel is important based on who you are becoming.  Your growth is not dictated by what you have been; your growth is determined by what you are becoming.

This point is very important and one not to skip over too quickly.  "What you have been" when it all began was an unidentified part of a whole — a very beautiful whole called God/Goddess/All That Is.  "What you are becoming" is a fully-identified and self-realized part of a beautiful God/Goddess/All That Is.  Which do you think is your source of motivation?  Obviously, it is what you are becoming.

You split off from your Oneness in search of yourself.  You were a spark, but you had no identity.  You broke away by your own free will to find yourself.  Once found, you return again to the Oneness.  You will be a spark again, only this time, knowing who you are, you will have an identity.  What motivates your growth?  The search for you and for your identity.  What motivates your growth?  Your future.

In each of these Kingdoms you experience The Source as a reminder of where you are going.  The Devas of the Mineral and Plant Kingdoms are the representation of The Love.  We would suggest that those of you who are strongly connected with these Kingdoms, having spent a relatively long time in either or each, can begin to understand the love that God/Goddess/All That Is has for you by touching the love the Devas have for the minerals and plants they guardian.

Notice the ease with which a rock will allow in God's love.  Notice how completely a plant will allow itself to be nurtured.  Notice the singular desire, expectancy, and imagining.  Notice the ultimate Dream of the Devas.

## *The Animal Kingdom*

After completing the initial Kingdoms, we would suggest, as consciousness you jump to the Animal Kingdom.  For the most part, you enter on a rather unsophisticated level of this Kingdom.  Usually you begin as a single-celled organism.  In the Animal Kingdom, there is the experience of reincarnation, so you do evolve to more sophisticated levels, and usually fairly rapidly.  As you create the illusion of living and dying, you learn.  Pulled by what you are becoming, pulled by your future, you learn.  Exploring, stretching and reaching, you learn and grow and become more of who you are.

After each animal lifetime, as consciousness again you evaluate and make choices and decisions.  We would suggest that the choices and the discernment provide the bases for the next round of incarnational experiences.  You progress up the ladder of evolution following your own path, which will eventually lead you to what seems like the epitome of all growth: The Human Kingdom.

Once you move out of any Kingdom, you never go back. Once you step over the boundary and enter the Human Kingdom, you never step back. Certain Eastern philosophies notwithstanding, you do not step back. The last animal lifetime, however, is a very important transitional lifetime. Within each animal species certain types of animals have a much smoother transition than others. In the species of birds, for example, we would suggest that an eagle, hawk, or owl has an easier transition to the Human Kingdom than, say, a buzzard! There is no species better than another; there are just certain animals within a species that are more likely to make the jump than others.

The last animal you were, we would suggest, is often your Spirit Animal. If you can remember or discover what it was, it can be of grand assistance in your current growth. It can be of assistance, that is true, but certainly it is not necessary to your growth.

## *The Human Kingdom*

Even when you enter the Human Kingdom you do not begin as a Rhodes Scholar or anything like that. Your first Human lifetimes, we would suggest, would undoubtedly be a source of embarrassment now. The best way to describe your first foray into Humanness would be to suggest that you were a Human Animal, not really a Human Being at all.

Your life was one of survival. You lived today and did what was necessary to get through today so you could live tomorrow. There was no hope or vision; there was just surviving. You existed. You existed just to exist.

You lived lifetime after lifetime like this. We call these lives your "pilot-light" lifetimes. You had enough life to keep lukewarm, to keep the pilot light burning, but not enough to really "get cookin'." There was plenty of friction — plenty of struggle and hardship. However, struggle and hardship are not the requisites of growth. A requirement of growth is dreaming. There was no Dream.

At some point in your repetitive cycle of survival lifetimes, something happened. Something happened that caused the pilot light to burst into flame. Something happened to create the microcosm of that initial explosion of consciousness. Something happened, and you realized that there was more to life than just survival! You did not know what that something was, but it was out there, and you made a choice.

You made your first initial choice, and the Journey began. We call the specific lifetime in which you made that choice your First Directional Lifetime. It was the lifetime when you decided to grow. It was the lifetime that began the Journey, the journey you are still upon, the Journey Home.

That was the lifetime when you took the jump from being a Human Animal to becoming a Human Being. What specifically happened to wake you up is important to many. What is more important is that it happened. Be the incident large or small, it took courage because you were stepping outside of a very limiting consensus reality. What happened immediately after you took that step is not so important. What is important is that you took the step. You began to grow!

There is something more to life than just surviving, and you are going to find what that *something more* is. That began, we would suggest, an exploration that you are still exploring. Even though your directional lifetime occurred thousands of years ago, we would suggest, you are not slow or stupid. In the larger scope of things, you are moving relatively fast.

You embarked upon your Quest of finding that *something more*. You began to grow by developing your human "beingness." You learned that you could create having things.

### Beyond The Human Being

Once you become a human being, you realize that there is still *something more. There is more to life than just surviving* evolves into *there is more to life than just having*. There is a quality of being a human being that is more important than the quantity. As you seek that mysterious quality, you subtly move from being human to discovering the fullness of being a Human Being with potential. This is the second choice to grow. The third initial choice is to move from the Potential Human Being to becoming a Metaphysical Human Being.

Initially, some feel they must forgo the quantity of life to demonstrate their tenacity for seeking the quality. Eventually they will realize that such a demonstration is not necessary, and, we would suggest, they will allow themselves to have both the quantity and the quality of being both a human being and a metaphysical being.

There is one more initial choice. After you move beyond the state of Human Animal and the state of Potential Human Being to the state of Metaphysical Human Being, then you are ready to choose to be a Spiritual Human Being.

Long ago you chose to move beyond the Human Animal stage of development. In many of what you call past lifetimes you also chose to move beyond the Human Being with Potential stage. You have remade that choice in this lifetime, too.

In this lifetime you were taught by the consensus reality and its many proponents that hard work and the proper manners would get you what you wanted in life. If you did what "they" told you to do, then everything would work out. The Industrial Revolution, the printing press, upward mobility, and the American Way would give you everything you could possibly want. Or, we would suggest, if not everything you could want, at least everything you *should* want.

It did not work!

Some of you turned to the Human Potential Movement which promised to develop everything in you to maximize your potential. You were analyzed and "therapized." You were rolled and Rolfed. You changed your clothes, you changed your career, and you changed the food you ate. You had it "given to you," and you "got it." You bio-feedbacked and psycho-cybernetized. It worked, sort of.

You came seeking a better job, a new car, an exciting relationship, and better health — you wanted tangible success. You learned the proper outlook and in-look to make it happen. It did, sort of.

There was an emptiness to having all the things you wanted without the fun — without the power. You were running as fast as you could. It was not enough. You had what you thought you wanted, and it was not enough! It was not enough . . .

Reaching for the top of the Human Potential Movement, you discovered metaphysics and the world of the paranormal. Metaphysics: the study of the worlds that lie beyond and between the physical. More answers would be found here.

When the American Dream failed, others of you, we would suggest, leaped over the Human Potential Movement opting to be more private in the discovery of your potential. You read the books and magazines and reflected. More quietly, you came to the same conclusions. It was not enough. . . .

Dressing for success was appropriately replaced with learning to love yourself. Learning how to know the right people was replaced with learning to know the "child within" — and the adolescent, too! Intimidation was replaced with a new kind of learning and a new kind of technique — metaphysical learning and technique designed to help you take back your power.

We would suggest: Once you successfully learn how to create your own reality, once you really know — really know in the depth of your being — that you are the only one who will make your life work, once you "grok" that only you can decide exactly how well is well in your life, then you can honestly and humbly call yourself a metaphysician. Once you sense yourself as a metaphysician — and only you can know for sure — your life becomes full of meaning and understanding. You develop your skills of manifesting the reality you want.

As a Metaphysical Human Being, the quantity of aliveness and the quality of life is such that, without desperation, you gently turn your attention to the Life Focus. We prefer Life Focus to Purpose of Life. Of course, you may use whatever term you prefer. Purpose implies a certain lack of choice, as though someone decided and then assigned a purpose to you before you entered this physical world. Focus, on the other hand, implies more self-determination. As with a camera, you choose to focus on certain things with a wide-angle or a zoom lens. You can color your focus, and you can change it.

At a certain mystical point in the exploration of your metaphysics — at a special juncture in your Journey Home — you discover a new spirituality. You discover the New Age — the Age of Humanity and the Age of Consciousness — that exists inside of you.

To your surprise, the New Age is a personal revelatory experience with no specific beginning. It is a private celebration that happens somewhere deep in your consciousness. Though you are still a metaphysician, you are something more. You do not need to tell anyone or convince even yourself. You know. You just know . . .

This knowing, we would suggest, is the beginning of your private and personal New Age. It is the step beyond the Metaphysical Human Being into the beautifully unknown realm of the Spiritual Human Being.

It is when you finally realize that the *something more* that you have been seeking has been found. The *something more* that is beyond surviving, that is beyond just having, that is even beyond being — the *something more* is . . . .

The *something more* is you and your Dream. The *something more* is you, your Dream, and your relationship with God/Goddess/All That Is.

Just as you think you are at the end of your Journey, you gratefully realize that it is just beginning anew. Whereas you travelled alone, now you begin to learn to travel together. You begin a Spiritual Journey Home in a co-creating partnership with God/Goddess/All That Is.

Just when you fully realize you are alone — you're not!

## *Reviewing the Process of Growth Consciousness*

*Mineral Kingdom*                    *Spiritual Human Being*

*Plant Kingdom*                    *Metaphysical Human Being*

*Animal Kingdom*                    *Potential Human Being*

*Human Animal/Human Being Kingdom*

You begin as Consciousness without identity and you seek to know yourself with the Unfinished Question: *"Why?"* After a series of simultaneous and continuous explosions of consciousness you, as your Higher Self, generate form as Thought, Consciousness Units, Subatomic Particles, and Atomic Particles. We would suggest that at this point you are still Consciousness looking for a denser form.

You enter the Mineral Kingdom and learn what is right for you to learn. It is an individual process. Once complete, you move to a vertical form of density, the Plant Kingdom. Here again you learn what you decide is important to learn. When you are ready, you jump into a directionally mobile form of density, The Animal Kingdom. Through a maze of lifetimes you fit the pieces of a puzzle together. When enough pieces are fitted, you take what seems to be the ultimate step, The Human Animal Kingdom.

To this point, growth seems almost automatic. Your Higher Self, your Unconscious Self and your Subconscious Self bring you this far in the process of growth. Now, we would suggest, it is up to you. You must choose to grow from here on out. The choices, which have been happening more or less automatically, now must happen consciously.

## *The First Conscious Choice*

The first conscious choice is "There is more to life than just surviving — there is more to living than just surviving. I am going to find that *something more.*"

The Journey Home begins.  This is where you stop separating from God/Goddess/All That Is.  This is where you turn around and start heading Home.  Do you see?  This turnaround has to be conscious, or else growth is meaningless.  The automatic separation is necessary for your growth.  The conscious return is also necessary.  If the return were also automatic, you would be nothing but a robot.

When you are first born, you are umbilically connected to mother as the source of your life and of your being.  That cord is cut physically, and you are separate.  It takes you a few years to realize that you are not emotionally one with mother, however.  With this realization, you begin to grow on your own, consciously.

Mother ties your shoes until you push away and insist, "No, let me!" Though you are clumsy at first, it is important that you learn.  It is important that you do it on your own, consciously.

When someone loves you, really loves you, which would you prefer: That their love is a conscious choice or that it is an automatic instinctive response?  What do you suppose God/Goddess/All That Is prefers?

Though these analogies do not work perfectly — no analogy does (if it did, it would no longer be an analogy, it would be the real thing!) — hopefully they help us make our point about the necessity of the separation and of the conscious return.

That part of you that is God/Goddess/All That Is — your Higher Self — guides your separation and takes you as far as the First Conscious Choice.  That part of you takes you to the farthest point away from God/Goddess/All That Is, but you — the conscious you — has to decide to Go Home.

If the return were automatic, too, it would be meaningless.  The Journey Home is a conscious journey.

Remember:  You are a piece of The Source; you are a part of The Love.  You cannot lose that.  You can pretend you are separate, but you can never really be separate.  When your Higher Self takes you to the farthest point away from God/Goddess/All That Is, it knows it is an illusion.  It is an illusion!  Again, it is an illusion!

You pretend you are separate, but you can never really be separate.  Enlightenment is about ending the pretense — consciously!  Consciously!

When you consciously and completely stop pretending, you are one with The Love.

## A Subsequent Choice: Preparing for The Sacred Journey

The first conscious choice begins The Journey Home — it does not end it! The choice must be and is conscious, but you must make a number of other choices before you will stop pretending. Everyone in your reality has made the first choice. There are some *homo sapiens* who exist on your planet, perhaps, who are still Human Animals. Perhaps in some remote, unknown area, there are those who exist just to exist with no sense of the *something more*. They are isolated and not really a part of what you call your personal reality.

Those who are in your reality, however, all have taken the first step — all have made the first conscious choice. Even those who, by your assessment, do not seem to be on any kind of a journey at all have made the conscious choice to return to The Love. They may resist it. They may be afraid of it. They may deny it. They are still on the Path. We would suggest that even you have done each of these things yourself, from time to time. Everyone has made the initial conscious choice. We would suggest that not everyone has made the subsequent choices. The Journey Home begins with the first conscious choice. You prepare for The Sacred Journey with the subsequent choices.

## The Human Potential

The second conscious choice is "There is more to life than just having things — there must be a depth, a richness, a quality of life. I am going to find that *something more* — that quality of life."

The second choice leads to the fifth step of the process of growth — Potential Human Being. With the second choice, we would suggest, you begin to develop the fullness of the human potential. Some do/did it with a bang — The Human Potential Movement with all its trappings. Others do/did it with a whisper, privately discovering/uncovering who you are.

Developing human potential is learning that "right attitude" and "right outlook" and "right language" and "right physical image" — that the "right stuff" — is what makes reality work for you. The proponents were correct. Your history highlights the special individuals who demonstrate the fullness of the human potential. The Human Potential Movement said that each person has a human potential, not just the special few. Some develop it naturally; others can take specific steps to consciously develop that same potential.

The cornerstone of the Human Potential Movement is that by accessing human resources with the proper attitude and vitality, you can accomplish anything. Everyone goes through their own human potential movement whether it is a public trek with lots of fellow participants or a private exploration with no fanfare.

The public trek is often referred to as the Human Potential Movement (with capital letters), and it spawned many new concepts which are now part of your social culture. Concepts such as Management by Objective, Business Stress Reduction, Meditation for the Executive, Networking, and Time Management Systems are all part of the public trek of realizing the potential within each person.

Another term became popular in this public exploration of what was beyond "just having." The advocates applied it to almost anything that was vanguard without really knowing what the term meant. The term so popularized: The New Age.

The third conscious choice occurs when you have accessed the human resources with propriety and vitality, and it is still not enough. You do not know what is missing, but something is. You feel guilty. You should be satisfied. You feel restless instead. You are tired of looking for only the human potential. There must be something more than combining and re-combining more human resources. There must be something more than the "right stuff," because although it worked for awhile, it is not working now.

It is not working! One more course, one more seminar, one more massage just is not working. The human potential, though valuable, is not the full answer. There is something more. There is still something more. The urge burns.

## *The Metaphysical Potential*

The third conscious choice is the metaphysical choice. "I create my own reality." Yes, human resources and the "right stuff" can be helpful and useful, but they do not create your reality. You do. The human potentials are not the source of your success; rather, they are the raw materials that you use to create your happiness. You are the source of your success.

The Human Potential Movement, when applied properly, is vital in preparing people for the next step in their growth. Those true leaders of this all-important Movement are courageous people who know their responsibility is to access the personal human resources; that is, to access the raw materials that are within each person. The true leaders know their real job. All the encounter therapies from primal screaming to sensory deprivation were intended to open people to what was already inside of them. All the body work from Feldenkrais to Rolfing were initially aimed at helping people discover the raw materials within their own being. The true leaders know this.

Some who claim to be leaders are not. They tend to deify the technique — they tend to worship the system. For them, the means become the ends. The therapies, for example, are valued for the resources they are, rather than for the resources they access; that is, we would suggest, people are evaluated on which workshops and seminars they took rather than on the benefit received from, or on the impact of, those weekend retreats.

Many have become what we call "vinyl warmers." They are the ones who show up at workshops thinking that if they can afford the price of admission they will automatically learn the information. They are the ones who act as if keeping the vinyl on the hotel ballroom chair warm will bring enlightenment.

That you showed up, that you sat there, that you have the certificate to prove it becomes enough. That you have not changed, that you rely less and less upon your potential and more and more on the promised potential of a system — that you are empty and even afraid to admit the hollowness — matters not when the system becomes the message.

The leaders-who-are-not and the "vinyl warmers" who follow them give their power away to the Movement. Having the "right stuff" becomes more important than what you think or feel about yourself. It becomes more than you.

Often the ability to intimidate and manipulate — to use others — is the criterion upon which success is measured. To some, it does not matter if you are happy or even content as long as your "life is working." Your life is working if you follow the rules — their rules. If you are unhappy, do not ask why. Just get happy. Just do it!

The deification of technique and system causes many to get stuck in the "loop of the Human Potential Movement." Sadly, they never really figure out just what these human potentials they have been seeking really are. Coming up empty-handed, they declare that the Movement is over or that it never was.

Well, what are the human potentials anyway? They are your ability to make choices and then to make decisions out of those choices. We would suggest that they are your ability to think and feel and then to allow your thoughts and feelings to matter, to have impact, to make a difference. They are your ability to know your attitudes and beliefs consciously and your ability to change them at will. The real human potentials are the raw materials out of which you create your own reality.

Developing the Metaphysical Potential is recognizing the raw materials — recognizing your human potential — and learning to apply them with a new set of tools. Being a metaphysician is about learning to use the tools of creation together with raw materials. It is also about dynamically combining the tools and materials to manifest what you want in your reality. Being a metaphysician, we would suggest, is also more than just creating what you want in your reality. It is creating your reality — all of it — personally and globally. *intention + Prayer      +    feelings + Emotions*

The tools of creation: desire, imagination, and expectancy. That is it. There are no others. Those you consider the grandest and those you consider the least have only these tools with which to work. Whatever reality anyone creates, consciously or not, it is created by using these and only these tools. As much as you want to think those you deem more successful than you have some secret weapon or some special advantage, they do not.

The only difference is in the application. They apply the tools more diligently, with greater intention, and with greater vision. Those who are more successful than you work with the tools and the raw materials with a difference, perhaps, but we would suggest that they have no more resources and no more tools with which to work those resources than you do.

### Ultimate Motivation

The metaphysical potential is your potential to love yourself and then to love others. It sounds too simple we know; however, it is true. Your Metaphysical Potential is your capacity to love yourself first and then to love others enough to motivate yourself to use the tools and the materials to spontaneously create a loving reality.

You see, you can use the raw materials — your human potential — to create a "proper" reality or an "acceptable" reality, or even an "abundant" reality. The question becomes one of depth: How much love is in your reality? How much does your reality nurture you?

Using the raw materials and the tools of creation, you can create a facsimile or even a real reality of love, but if your motivation is "to do it because you are supposed to," then you are close, but still not there. "There" is when you create that loving reality spontaneously — without having even to think about it!  "There" is loving yourself and others so much and so automatically that you do not even have to plan your reality — it just happens as a celebratory reflection of your love!

You do not love yourself enough, yet, nor do you love others enough, yet, to do that.   Therefore, the metaphysical world is filled with techniques to use until you do.

Once you honestly love yourself completely and then others adequately — an ideal state admittedly — you will not need to know the techniques of reality creation, because you will create that reality automatically.   The automatic would be conscious, but automatic nonetheless.

Pause for a moment: The automatic would be conscious, but it would still be automatic.   You see, you begin your evolution of growth with automatic reality creation which is unconscious, and you ultimately return to automatic reality creation that is conscious!   You have created such an elegant world!

If you loved yourself completely, you would only create a positive reality. Out of total self-love, would you create hardship and pain?   Would you believe that others would suffer hardship and pain?   No.   You would instead create a world of total joy and happiness where you knew what you need to know to be personally and socially joyous and happy.

## The How's and Why's

Some are waiting for that utopian world of total self-love.   Until such time, however, it is important to learn the how's and why's of reality creation.

Some believe that such a utopia is impossible and that even to think such thoughts is an irresponsible waste of time.   They think — and some even honestly feel — that such idealism is not only irresponsible, it is downright dangerous.   We would suggest that we are not going to argue with them.   We would only say that if they are so sure they are correct, then they (even more than the people who are waiting for that perfect day) would be advised to learn the how's and why's of reality creation as quickly as possible!

The how's of reality creation are part of taking back your power. Knowing that there are the tools of desire, expectancy, and imagination is the first step.   Knowing how to use those tools, however, is power.   Accepting the raw materials is essential.   Consciously working and creating with them is power, personal power.   The how's of reality creation are what the "all of metaphysics" is about.

The why's of reality creation are another integral part of taking back your power.   We know that it is popular, particularly within certain elements of the Human Potential Movement, to say that you should not ask why.   You are told that "why" gets in the way of your experience.   You are told never to ask "why," only to ask "how."

Though you never ask why that is so, references are made to particular authorities who are partially quoted.  Most often Fritz Perls is credited as the author of this concept.  He would be chagrinned to hear how his ideas have been taken out of context to support a "pop psychology" that even he warned against.

Yes, asking this fatal question can take you away from the experience, but only if you ask what we call the "explaining why."  When asking the "understanding why," not only does it not take away from experience, it heightens it, and it engenders power, personal power.

What is the difference?  To the question *Why are you late?* there are two kinds of answers.  The "explaining why" deals with traffic lights and rush hours.  It deals with last-minute phone calls and cars that never start, and it deals with time that got away and idiosyncratic behavior.  All of this does take away from the experience.

The "understanding why," however, deals with reluctance and resistance to getting together.  It deals with martyrhood, frustration, and guilt for always being this way.  It deals with a self-image and a level of self-love and love for others.  These admissions are not as noble — that is true — but they are more empowering.  It may be unpleasant to talk about some of these issues, but such a discussion might, just might, produce change — conscious change — that can only come from fully understanding, not explaining, why.

As another example of what we mean:  So often you know exactly what you need to do to be happy.  You even know how to do it, but, for some reason that you do not understand, you just cannot do it.  "It" may be simple or intricate.  It does not really matter.  You just cannot.  You just cannot.  You just . . .

You just do not understand why, and therefore, with "how's" spilling out of the top of your head and with "experience you are in touch with" up to your eyebrows, you are powerless.  You will remain powerless even if the current crisis passes, until you understand (not explain) why.

The "explaining why's" do take you away from experience and do take you away from knowing that you do create your own reality.  The "explaining why's" make it look like reality creates you.  The "explaining why's" leave you feeling as if you have nothing to do with creating the world you experience.

The "understanding why's," though empowering, are vulnerable and self-disclosing, sometimes awkward and embarrassing, and not the easiest party conversation, especially when the party's purpose is to intimidate and manipulate your way to success.  Therefore, we would suggest, it is neither surprising nor any wonder that many have attempted to eliminate the potentially pesky "why."

In fact, when you work with the "understanding why's" you experience that you do, indeed, create your own reality. You become powerful. If you only know how and do not understand why you created a particular reality, you will never fully know whether you can re-create it (or keep from re-creating it) in the future. You may comprehend how to do or not do again, but you will not understand your initial, or subsequent motivation for implementing those how's.

In lieu of total self-love and love for others, you learn how's and why's of reality creation. You also learn that you create it all. There is no one out there who will do it for you. You are alone in doing it for yourself.

The fear of loneliness deters many a potential metaphysician. Before you can move on, though, you must come to this conclusion on your own. We would suggest that not only must you come to it alone, you must experience it totally before you will allow yourself to know the secret. You must own it totally before you will give yourself permission to be eligible to make the fourth conscious choice.

## The Spiritual Human Being

When you know — not just suspect — that you are the only one who creates not only your reality but all of reality, then you are ready. When you know — not just suppose — that everything in your world and on the physical plane has been created by you, you are coming very close to a new level of awareness. Even though you may not know all the how's and why's, even though you are not totally proficient in using the tools of creations, and even though you lack elegance in dealing with the raw materials of your reality, if you know — really know — that it is you who is doing it all, then your are ready for the secret.

The Secret: You are not really alone. There is a Source; there is a Love; there is a God. We would suggest that there is a God/Goddess/All That Is.

The fourth conscious choice comes from the intricacy of several realizations. First, that there is more to life than just surviving; second, that there is more than just having things; third, that although you create it all, and you know it, there is something even more important. The fourth choice is "Whatever that *something more* is, I am going to find it."

That *something more* is you and your Dream. It is your spirituality. Beyond having and beyond creating it all yourself, and the satisfaction and power that these awarenesses entail, there is your spirituality. This is the *something more* that moves you into the seventh step of your growth. It moves you into the realm of being the Spiritual Human Being.

That *something more* is finally discovering a self that is more self than you have ever known. It is discovering a self that already has a living, breathing, loving, embracing relationship with God/Goddess/All That Is. It is discovering, exploring, and then living a fully spiritual life.

What is a fully spiritual life? Answering that question is what the journey is really all about. There is no one answer that can be definitively written or stated. Individually, each of you must find out how to define the "spiritual life" and then live it for yourself. You, each of you, will, in fact, find out. You will live it for yourself — eventually.

Many will conjure pictures of their childhood religion when they think of spirituality and instantly say, "No, thank you!" Many of you became involved in metaphysics through the human potential door to get away from the pain, loneliness, and guilt that you have correctly or incorrectly associated with traditional religion. You leave the past and its traditional religion behind, and you think you have walked away from your spirituality. When you encounter the concept of spirituality in your growth, rather than seeing a relationship with God, you tend to see your old pictures of traditional religion, but you call it spirituality.

Spirituality is your relationship with The Source, with The Love, with God/Goddess/All That Is. That relationship may be good or bad, indifferent or non-existent. No matter, it is still your spirituality. The most confirmed atheist has a relationship with God/Goddess/All That Is, and therefore has a spirituality.

The pictures in your inner child's mind are pictures of a limiting traditional spirituality that is based on the consensus reality. To some, the images are of Sunday school and church, of lengthy sermons and hushed boredom pitted against an almost uncontrollable urge to run and shout and play. It is pews too hard and stubby pencils too dull. It represents all the duty and obligation you tried to avoid as a child.

To others, the images are of stuffy piety shrouded in arrogance and superiority. Even the word evokes pictures of angry righteousness cloaked in self-pity. It is synonymous with the hypocrisy and imprisonment of the organized religion of childhood. Still for others, the pictures are of sticky sweetness amidst a mire of convoluted and complex doctrine and dogma. It is hushed breathy tones that impotently cover the alienation and loneliness, or the fear and bitterness, of the negative ego's broken promise.

This kind of spirituality is what you ran away from when you began your Journey Home. Now it sounds like you are running right back into it! This is why many people will not take this step. This is why so many still shrink from dealing with their spirituality.

There are three directions to take. Some have taken each.

The first direction: You can hold the old pictures and create a consensus-reality spirituality all over again like the new Fundamentalist Christians are attempting to do. The resurgence of Fundamentalism through the electronic religion of television evangelism is not really that surprising. People made the initial decision to grow and progressed on their Journey Home. Even as they resist and deny, they have made that choice. When they insist on holding onto the old pictures, they will naturally return to the old spirituality with a new vigor. They become "born again."

A second alternative: You can reject the pictures and reject any possibility of a true spirituality. You can create a false spirituality headed by a non-god with non-followers taught by non-teachers all of whom are not responsible for anything. Under the umbrella of the Human Potential Movement or the Metaphysical Potential Movement, many have taken this tack. They have vociferously and prolifically laid forth their non-doctrine for all to non-judge. Much of the criticism of metaphysics, spirituality, and of the New Age is actually leveled against those who have chosen this second alternative.

Because these few have spoken so loudly, so frequently and so outlandishly, they have been erroneously considered the spokespersons for and leaders of a public movement that is, in truth, a very personal journey. It is ironic that a small of group people, who are actually terrified of making the spiritual jump because they will not let go of the "pictures of the past," consider themselves and are considered by the consensus reality to be the leaders of the New Age. You are the leaders. Each of you individually is the leader of your Journey Home.

The third and preferred alternative is to recognize the pictures from your childhood for what they are. Own them as yours, and own that you created them. Forgive yourself. Then change the pictures of spirituality to the new pictures. Realize that the spiritual life is a life seeking new pictures — it is a life seeking a new relationship with God/Goddess/All That Is.

The spiritual life is ever-changing and ever-expanding. Once you find new pictures, realize that they too will become old and yellowed. When that happens — tomorrow, next week, next year, or in the next decade — be willing to give the pictures up and to get new ones. The face of God/Goddess/All That Is is continuously changing. Get new pictures.

One of the major problems with spirituality is that people want to trap God/Goddess/All That Is. The scientists attempt to catch The Source in a mathematical formula on a dusty chalkboard or in the maze of computer solid state. The theologians look in the pages of some Holy Books or in the syllogisms of some inductive or deductive reasoning. The philosophers seek God by whatever name by evaluating and reevaluating the nature of humankind. The doctors look inside each cell. The seekers try to systematize "The Love" in useless attempts to guarantee that it will always be there.

God/Goddess/All That Is will never be proved. The Love will never be trapped, because it is always changing, expanding, and growing. When you find a system of spirituality, know that it will become obsolete. Growth is about defining and "busting" systems that are to be replaced with new systems which will, in turn, be defined and "busted" and similarly replaced, etcetera, etcetera, etcetera.

The third alternative is to become a Spiritually Alive Human Being who is continuously seeking, finding, and then seeking all over again, a new and deeper loving relationship with a very personal and caring God/Goddess/All That Is. This is the final journey.

This is the Sacred Journey Home.

Welcome . . .

# *Part III*
## *The Steps of Getting There*

*"When seeking Truth — when honestly seeking your truth — always remember: The steps of getting there are always the same as the qualities of being there."*

*—Lazaris*

# THREE

## *The Journey Begins: Love*

So where are you? Much farther along on your journey than you think! Many lifetimes ago you realized that there was more to life than just surviving. Each of you has already experienced your First Directional Lifetime. You have experienced many, many lifetimes of spectacular growth and illumination. This is not the first time you have discovered the human potential that lies within you, nor the first time you have learned of your metaphysical potential, either. The spiritual journey is one that you have begun — or at least attempted to begin — many times before.

Each of your many lifetimes has the potential of being the one that leads you Home. The fact that you are here would suggest that in those lifetimes you call previous lives, you have not yet chosen — you have not yet decided — to go Home. That is quite all right, because you have this one — this lifetime — where you can make that choice! You can make it now.

You see, we would suggest that this lifetime happens to be like a microcosm of your growth. In this current experience of physicalness, you have also come to the conclusion that there is more to life than surviving, and that there is more than just "having" as well. You have discovered your human potential publicly or privately. We would suggest that you may not use all your potential, that is true, but it is available to you like it never has been at any other time in the history of consciousness. Whether you use it or not, there is technique — there are ways to fully access your human potential.

For each of you, the details of your metaphysics may vary a little or a lot. Regardless of the variations, you have discovered your metaphysical potential as well.

Don't wait!

You are at the final of The Four Choices To Grow. You are ready to explore the Spiritual Potential — you are ready to explore The Sacred Journey. You can almost feel the push-pull of this realization. Yes, you know you are there. You know you are ready. In many ways you have already begun. Yet you can feel the fear that says, "No, not yet! I'm not ready! I need more time!"

Remember that special Friday night party? What about the anticipation of the first day of vacation? You wanted it so badly you could taste it! Then it arrived. Do you remember how you felt? Excited. Relieved. And you felt a strange emptiness — a hollowness that seemed to haunt you. There was a sadness. There was fear.

Like that first day of vacation or the Friday night party, the Sacred Journey has been a goal for so long — it has been a Dream for so many lifetimes — that you want to keep it a goal or a Dream forever. As the status changes from goal to achievement, there is a reluctance. There is a fear that says, "Not yet!"

You decided not to turn back to a traditional spirituality of your childhood. For some that is an important path — for some that is the proper path. You decided it was not for you.

Some of you have already been down the second alternative road far too many times even to want to count. Through the late '60's, most of the '70's and the early '80's, you examined the non-spirituality with the non-teachers with their limited non-points-of-view.

You got hurt. You fell and often felt foolish. People about whom you cared, and people you thought cared about you, laughed and turned away. They often dismissed you. You were ridiculed and criticized. You were considered irresponsible and non-accountable and even dangerous by a consensus reality that would not — perhaps could not — understand.

You kept picking yourself up again and dusting yourself off. You kept trying a new path, a new workshop, or a new special meeting that was "guaranteed" to produce "instant enlightenment." Then, when "instant" took too long, or made you look shallow, you found some newer group promising that your enlightenment would take forever! In fact, you were told, maybe you never would make it. The doors were closing soon, you were told, and those that made it, would. Those who did not, would not! Many followed the teachers and the non-teachers down one too many paths of non-spirituality. They gave up. In pain, they turned their backs upon growth.

Too many roads that ended. Too many roads.

## *The Sadness*

For many the sadness is that they were motivated by their own negative ego. While your consciousness was falling and hurting and turning away, your negative ego was "going for it" — "it" being any negative ego payoff it could find. Its agenda in joining one of the non-groups may well have been to have someone to blame: "It's the group's fault. . . . They misled me. . . .They taught me the wrong stuff in the wrong way. . . ." Perhaps the negative ego was seeking the self-pity and/or the self-importance that is often associated with the "blind alleys" of metaphysics. Certain groups or disciplines are built upon the premise that "no one understands us," and thus "poor us" is mixed with the "better-than" of an exclusivity. Some negative egos loved the jargon of many non-groups because only "fellow members" (we use the word "fellow" advisedly) would understand. Again there is the double edge. On one side the negative egos feel "better than" because only they know what is being said. On the other side, they feel sorry for themselves because no one else can understand them!

While your Spiritual Self stumbled and was ridiculed, your negative ego was holding out for manipulative power — was holding out for the short-cut to enlightenment. Power is the ability and the willingness to act. Power has nothing to do with instilling fear, or with intimidation, or with the ability to overpower.

Yet so often you define power in these terms. So often someone scares you or overpowers you, and you do not admit your fear and humiliation. Instead you envy their "power." A truly powerful person does not always have to be telling you how powerful they really are. They do not need to rely upon manipulative means to control their reality — or to control you, which is often what the powermongers are really after. Power is the ability and the willingness to act.

Your negative egos were looking for the secret of controlling others. They just called it a path of enlightenment. In the process of rejecting the old pictures of spirituality, in the process also of rejecting any sense of a real spirituality in favor of a false spirituality with its Non-God deity, in the process of taking this second alternative as your fourth essential choice of growth, you ended up abandoning your real self who, ironically, was the only one who ended up controlled. That is the sadness.

## *The Pain*

For many the pain is that they were motivated by a sincere and beautiful desire to grow. You are beautiful in your eagerness and your earnestness. If anyone even hinted at an opportunity of growth — if anyone even suggested that they had something you needed to know — we would suggest that you were beautifully right there willing to grow. Too often, you ended up being used. Some of you really were misled and taken advantage of. Since it was not your negative ego's payoff, you really were hurt. However, you kept going back for more, not because you were so stupid as many would want to have you believe, but because you were so sincere and, yes, so naïve. You were told not to judge, but you were also taught not to discern! Your hungry heart blinded you. That is the pain.

You are waking up more and more. You have declined the first alternative of spirituality. You have stumbled and bumped your way through the second alternative. Forgive yourself. It's time.

You are ready for the third: To create new pictures, to create a new relationship with God/Goddess/All That Is. You are ready for the Sacred Journey.

Don't wait!

## *The Beginning: Love*

You have heard it so often. Almost every "self-help" and "how-to" book tells you that the secret to whatever they are helping you to do is love. There are usually some glowing paragraphs that end with the wisdom that *you need to love yourself more.*

"Is that it? Is that all that is going to be said?" you wonder. Most often, yes! Everyone tells you to love yourself more. Some go further to tell you to love others, also. Very few actually tell you how to do it. How do you love? What are the specific steps?

Now your negative ego comes alive. It jumps in with a very loud, "No! Love should be a mystery." It says, "Don't de-mystify love. If it's real, it will just happen. You don't need to learn about love, just do it!" To ensure that you will not inquire further, it adds, "If you have to learn to love, you'll ruin it. If you have to learn to love, something is wrong with you."

You swallow hard. Sheepishly, you read on in the book pretending *you need to love yourself more* is something you never really knew before. "How profound," you lie to yourself.

The truth: You knew you needed to love yourself more. That's why you started reading the book in the first place! You know what you need to do. You do not always know how to do it.

The Sacred Journey does begin with love. Admittedly, it is a cliché. Because you have heard it before, your negative ego can say you are not learning anything new here.

Well, we suppose we could say the Sacred Journey begins with covering your body with mustard and ketchup. That would satisfy your ego — you certainly have not heard that before! That it is untrue is of no consequence to the negative ego. It is new and exciting and something different. "Who cares about the truth?" says the negative ego.

We are not here to entertain your negative ego. We return to the cliché about love. Sometimes a cliché is a cliché because it is an over-used phrase. Sometimes it is a cliché because it is a real and understood truth. The truth is a cliché because it is the truth.

The Sacred Journey does begin with love. It begins with self-love and does expand into loving others. The Sacred Journey involves giving love, receiving love, and — for many a new concept — being loved.

Whether you can do it or not, you know what giving and receiving love are about. *Being loved* is opening yourself up and allowing yourself to change — to really change — because someone loves you. "I am changing because they love me." The "they" can be anyone.

It is most magical and mystical when that "they" is your own Higher Self. "I am changing . . . I am changing because my Higher Self loves me." You really need no other motivation.

You already know why it is important to love. But why is love important in your relationship with God/Goddess/All That Is? The obvious: If you do not love yourself, you will not be willing to let yourself be loved by anyone, especially by All That Is. Without loving others, how can you love the most significant other there is?

The not-so-obvious: Love is an emotion and a state of being. It is both a feeling and a level of awareness. Further, it is the only feeling/awareness that transmutes, transforms, and transcends all energy. It is universal. It is the only feeling/awareness that transmutes, transforms, and transcends every level of consciousness. *Love is the only "line of communication" that reaches all the way to God/Goddess/All That Is.*

## A Feeling or An Awareness?

There are those who contend that love is a feeling — just a feeling and no more. They say it is temporal, ever-changing, always expanding or contracting.

At the same time, another philosophy states that love is not a feeling at all. Rather, love is a state of consciousness that is constantly sought, but never fully found.

In fact, we would suggest that love is both. It is a feeling that you can spontaneously explore, and it is a skill that you can specifically learn. There is the skill and art of loving.

Love is also an ideal. It is a state of awareness, a state of being or consciousness that you are always seeking. Though you will never fully embrace the totality of love, in your search, while you stretch and reach, you become more and more of the ideal you pursue. You become more and more the very love you seek.

## It Is Universal

Transmute, transform, transcend? More New Age jargon? No, they are all three very important concepts that play an integral part in your growth. They are often defined with the usual "you know" metaphysical definitions which tell you nothing and often leave you more confused than ever. Well, we are not going to deal with everything these three concepts represent, but a cursory definition is perhaps in order.

You are standing at a vending machine clutching a ten-dollar bill. Try as you might, you cannot fit the bill into the coin slot. You may even have enough money to buy every candy bar or soft drink in the dumb machine, but with a ten-dollar bill you are impotent. You go get change. An attendant gives you a five, four ones, and change! Blessed change!

*Transmutation is changing something from one form to another like-form that is of equal intrinsic value, but is more useful and thus more personally valuable.* The ten-dollar bill is one form and the five, four ones and change are a like-form. They are still money, and they have the same intrinsic value, but one form is far more useful and thus more valuable to you.

You may feel angry, hurt, and scared. You might withdraw and protect yourself by being stubborn and defensive — stuck. You are impotent. Try as much as you want, and you still get nowhere. You can work your techniques and do your meditations and call upon your higher or inner guidance, and nothing much happens at all. Each of you has been in that place more than you want to admit right now. You have been there. You cannot change anymore than you can get the ten-dollar bill into the coin slot!

If you will transmute the stubbornness into determination and the defensiveness into openness, then you can move! Then your techniques and meditations can work! Then you can also transmute the deeper feelings as well.

You can change them from one form (emotion) to another like-form (another emotion), but the new form (determination and openness) is much more useful and valuable to you. You might think that stubbornness and determination are not of like-form. That's because determination is consistently more useful to you than stubbornness. It is easy to confuse intrinsic value with personal value. An emotion is an emotion. Even though some are more valuable to you than others, they are still of like-form with equal intrinsic value.

Emotions are emotions. Therefore, transmuting emotion is changing it from one emotion to another emotion that is far more useful and valuable to you at the time. Love is the most powerful energy for transmuting. If you remember the love, you can more easily transmute any less useful emotion into any more useful one.

Once you have transmuted the ten-dollar bill into a five, four ones and change, you can now purchase the soft drink. Once you actually make the purchase — once you put the coins in the slot and push or pull the buttons and hear that all-too-familiar sound of the aluminum can dropping out — you have now witnessed transformation.

You now have a five, four ones and an aluminum can! Ninety per cent of the bills are still in their transmuted form. They are still in like-form and equal to 90% of the ten-dollar bill, but the change has been transformed into a soft drink, into carbonated liquid in a can.

*Transformation is changing something from one form to a different form — an "unlike-form" — that is intrinsically of different value, though more personally useful and thus more personally valuable.* The intrinsic value can be more or less, just so it's different. You cannot say that the aluminum can is truly more valuable than a dollar's worth of change, but you can say its value is different! In fact, once you drain the contents, most would agree that though certainly transformed, it is of less value.

The stubbornness and defensiveness that cover the anger, hurt, and fear are transmuted into determination and openness, and transformed into drive and action. Drive and action are unlike-forms — they are doingness rather than beingness — and their value is also different. They become much more personally valuable, as any of you know who have felt very determined but had no drive, had no will. You have each felt very open and vulnerable, but the lack of action has left you empty and hollow. To move something from its potential state to its actual state is the process of transformation. Good intentions can result from transmuting the destructive to the productive, but permanent change comes with manifestation — with dynamic manifestation — of those intentions. Permanent change comes with transformation.

Being willing to give love and being willing to receive love are the greatest motivators, the greatest fuel, of transformation. Being loved — letting someone love you — is the most mystical and magical power of transformation.

Holding the frosty cold can to your lips, tipping your head back and drinking, you are now witnessing transcendence. You have transmuted a piece of paper into metal tokens called coins of equal value. You have transformed that paper into an aluminum can and a carbonated liquid which many would say is bad for your health.

Now . . . a ten-dollar bill has just quenched your thirst! That's transcendence!

*Transcendence is changing something from one form to a higher octave form that is intrinsically and personally more valuable. Transcendence is changing something from one form to a greater form that allows you to be more of who you are.*

A ten-dollar bill suddenly is a thirst-quencher — a higher octave or a greater form. All would agree that something that quenches your thirst — physically or emotionally — is both intrinsically and personally more valuable.

The drive transcends into success, and the action moves to its higher octave of positive impact. Stubbornness and defensiveness become successful action with positive impact. That is transcendence. With transcendence, you do not always know "how to get there from here." With transcendence, you sometimes don't think you are ever going to make it, but you do.

Transcendence is allowing miracles into your life. Let more miracles happen. Love is the guarantee in the world of no guarantees! Love allows miracles.

## *Open Line of Communication*

On the physical plane, you have access to the full range of positive and negative emotion. Positive and negative can have at least two distinct meanings. On one hand, they can mean good and bad, and on the other, they can be interpreted as *yin* and *yang*, or contracting and expanding, without a judgment of right or wrong. For the most part, the consensus reality agrees that feelings like love, joy, happiness, excitement, etc., are positive — they are good. Likewise, anger, hurt, sadness, fear, etc., are universally considered negative or bad emotions.

Metaphysicians have often adopted the consensus reality interpretation by saying you should feel the good emotions all of the time and never feel the bad ones. Often one's metaphysical or spiritual prowess is measured by the presence of good and the absence of bad emotions so defined by the consensus.

We would offer a more intricate view. Positive emotions are the ones that are appropriately expressed and released. Negative emotions are not appropriately expressed and/or released. The emphasis is on "appropriately." Sometimes that may mean direct expression — talking to the person or resolving the situation directly in your physical world. Sometimes that may mean indirect expression — talking to the person or playing through the situation in meditation.

Hate that is expressed and released appropriately is a very "positive" emotion, while its suppression and sublimation is very "negative" and can be very dangerous. On the other hand, love which is denied and turned inward can become twisted and destructive. It can become murderous. People have been killed out of hate (Martin Luther King, Jr.), and they have been killed out of love (John Lennon), but no one has been killed when that hate or love was appropriately expressed and released.

The other differentiation of emotion is more clearly between expanding and contracting emotion. This delineation conforms more completely with the concepts of *yin-yang*. Those emotions which expand your awareness are positive, and those which contract your awareness are negative. They are, however, neither good or bad. Every emotion begins with the option of being expansive or contracting. Then, as you mature, your emotions stabilize.

For example, there is a time in your evolution when the expression of anger and hurt are very expansive, and therefore should be called positive. However, after a certain level of advancement, anger and hurt are not bad, but they are contracting. Eventually, they become only contracting, and you drop them off. You drop them off not because they are bad or wrong, but because they are contracting and your growth — your spiritual evolution — has reached the level where it is all expansive. That occurs, however, once you have expanded beyond the physical plane.

In our reality, for example, we know anger, but we never feel it. We know hurt, fear, and despair, but we never feel them. They are contracting emotions, and there is no room for them in our ever-expanding reality. Though we do not ever feel these negative emotions — these contracting emotions — we can know what you go through when you do.

On your physical plane you have access to all emotion. As you grow and move to higher levels, the suppressed and potentially twisted emotions drop away. The contracting emotions also drop off. The last of the negative emotions is the fear of loneliness. It finally drops away, too.

The expressed and expansive emotions do just that — they express and expand to fill the void. Eventually even the range of positive emotion changes. The range converges. It becomes more focussed and more concentrated. Eventually the only emotion left is love.

It is then that love, the feeling, becomes Love the State of Being, the State of Consciousness. It is only then that Love is God/Goddess/All That Is.

The one fully open line of communication between you and God/Goddess/All That Is is the line of love that becomes Love — or should it be LOVE?

## The Skill & The Art of Loving

Love is a state of doing and being. There are some very specific things to do in order to love either yourself or others. The doing is the same. The direction changes, that's all.

From behind the mask of negative ego, you want to make loving difficult so you can justify and rationalize the lack of it in your life. After all, in your Faustian relationship with your negative ego, you have convinced yourself that if you let it run your life, it will deliver everything. Negative ego never delivers love. The only thing it does deliver is unkept and broken promises. It never delivers love.

"Where is the love?" you ask, and your ego tells you how hard — how impossible — it is. Your negative ego tells you how much love hurts.

When you find out just how available love really is, you either want to deny it completely as you protect your negative ego's position — "Avoid humiliation at all costs!" sayeth your negative ego — or you feel so stupid for having shut love out for so long that you do not think you deserve it now. Either way, you (not your ego) lose.

When you discover just how easy it is, do not run away. Do not punish yourself. Do not postpone it any longer. Start loving!

The things to do for love:

1.  Give.   Start giving to yourself and others in as many ways as you can. Give physically, emotionally, intellectually, and intuitively. Do not worry about getting . . . just really develop your ability to give.

2.  Respond.   Allow yourself the ability and the willingness to respond. Be responsible to yourself and then to others.

3.  Respect.   Honor your emotions and the emotions of the others who you want to love. Respect is not an issue of doing. It is a issue of honoring. So often when people try to gain respect from themselves or others they look around for something to do. They then work hard at doing whatever it is they decided would give them respect only to discover that their respect level has not really changed. They feel like failures. To respect yourself is to honor your emotions. You honor emotions by appropriately expressing and releasing them. You honor other people's emotions by giving the permission and safe space for them to express and release what they honestly feel. To love, honor your feelings. Honor the feelings of others.

4.  Know.   There are two ways of knowing someone — through inflicting pain or through seeking understanding. Because so many are afraid of love, they inflict pain — on themselves and on others. Your therapists, through psychological studies of surviving prisoners of war, know that an interesting, if not bizarre, relationship developed between captive and captor. Through the pain, they came to know each other more deeply than either anticipated.

Yes, one route of knowing is through pain, but there is another route. Seeking understanding begins with a conscious desire and concludes with a conscious commitment. It involves taking the time to really reach out — tenderly, to reach out . . . to develop the skill of loving, seeking understanding of yourself and others. You are not in this world to be understood. You are here to be understanding.

5.  Have the Humility to be Intimate.   Humility is the willingness to see each day as being brand new. It is the willingness to let people change instead of insisting that they can never change. You create your reality primarily out of choice and belief. If you consistently choose to see people at their worst and believe that, then that is just the way they are. You will be

right, but miserable.  To be humble is to say, "That's the way it's always been, and it can be different now."  Be humble enough to be close, tender, and vulnerable with yourself and with those about whom you care.

6.  Have the Courage to Commit.  Commitment is really frightening to many of you.  Fear of rejection and humiliation are the major culprits.  Fear of responsibility — "can I handle it?" — contributes massively to your refusal to be committed.  To many, commitment feels like imprisonment.  They confuse obligation with responsibility.  When you consider committing yourself to another, often your negative ego steps in with the question, "If you can create it this good, couldn't you do better?  Don't commit.  Wait!"  It admonishes you not to commit, saying that someone or something better just might show up.  If the better does show up, you still wait.  Commitment never comes.  It takes courage to love.

7.  Care.  Honestly begin to care for yourself and how your life is going.  We did not say "feel sorry for yourself."  Love has nothing to do with self-pity.  We said care.  You do not need a reason to care.  Just open your heart and your mind and begin.  Let yourself care for yourself.  Let yourself care for others.

These are the seven things to do in order to love.  You know each of them, and you have done them all from time to time.  In fact, you do know how to love.  You just don't think you do.

There is more to it than this, though.  You do these seven things in order to accomplish something.  It is the dynamic between doing these seven things with the express purpose of providing the following that creates love:

1.  Security.  Physical, emotional, intellectual, and intuitive safety for yourself or for another.  This is where love begins.

2.  Pleasure.  To give, respond, respect, or know yourself or someone else so as to provide them with short- and long-term pleasure — to be intimate, to be committed, and to care for yourself or another so that you or they feel safe.

3.  Honesty & Vulnerability.  To make it all right to let down the walls of defense.  To let it be all right to be totally open and honest.  To provide the space to expose your anxieties and doubts without fear.

4.  Trust.  A most powerful energy you can give yourself.  A most beautiful gift for others.

5.  Reduced Fear of Loss.  If you had a dazzling gold ring that you thought was just an inexpensive alloy plated with gold, you would wear the ring anywhere and everywhere without fear.  Now you find out that the ring is pure gold, and a very rare gold at that, and that it cannot be replaced.

Suddenly you want to lock up the ring. You are afraid of wearing it anywhere. The fear of losing something so valuable is terrifying.  When you love someone all fears evaporate, except one.  The fear of loss is the only fear that increases as love increases.  When you really love, the value increases.  If you were to lose that love now . . . it would be devastating!  If you love more, the value only increases and the fear of losing only increases.  This is why many of you run from love, or why some even stop loving.  Ironically, the antidote to this fear of loss is to take a deep breath and love more.  The answer is to take a deep breath and give, respond, respect . . . and care!  For love to be more than a word, it should work at reducing the very fear it produces.

6.  Intimacy and Caring.  Act in such a way so as to create a resonance of closeness and tenderness, to create a resonance of freedom and safety.

7.  Knowing.  To communicate — to be empathic.  Let the other know that you know them.  Let them know you see their beauty, and the not-so-beautiful side, and you love them anyway.  With self-love admit your strength and love it.  Admit your weakness.  Admit your ugliness, and love it. Quite so, it is easy to love the beauty, and it's the ugliness that needs the love, too.

You see, you do not just give, respond, or respect just to do it.  You do these things to provide security and pleasure, or honesty and vulnerability.

By understanding the seven things to do and the potential states of being to provide, you can know if you are loving yourself and others.  You can know if others are loving you.  Are you feeling loved?  Are they doing these things to produce the states of being called love?

Always begin with yourself.  Start with yourself in practicing your doing and being of love.  Then expand to include others — not just any others, but specific others, significant others.  Once you have developed the skill, once you are really good at loving, then expand that love even further.  As you expand the circle of love, always intensify self-love and the love for those special others.

The beginning: Love.  The first step of the Sacred Journey, and the first quality of being on the journey, begins with Love, with reaching and stretching for Love . . . for LOVE.

# FOUR

## *The Journey Continues: The Middle Steps*

The Sacred Journey begins with love. However, there is more than love. There are other steps to take, other qualities of being the spiritually alive person on your final journey — on your Sacred Journey Home.

These middle steps are often overlooked. You know the importance of love. You have an idea, albeit only an inkling, as to the importance of developing a relationship with your Higher Self. The middle steps often seem like something you should put off until you have more time. Some will decide they need to get their lives together first. They need to hurry up and get that relationship with their Higher Self really "humming," and then they can get around to dealing with the details.

In fact, it is the middle steps that will prepare you to really meet your Higher Self. Anyone can go on a meditation. Anyone can take you on a meditation to meet your Higher Self. Because you are eager, because you desire so much to grow, you will meet someone or something. Is it your Higher Self? Is it really? How do you know?

If you take the middle steps, if you develop the middle qualities, then you will know. The middle steps will prepare you in such a way that when you meet your Higher Consciousness, you will know it is real. You will not have to wonder if you are not just seeing another, perhaps more attractive, mask of your negative ego.

We have taken thousands of people to love and be loved by their Higher Selves. No matter how skeptical of their own ability, each has reached out and touched the hand of their Higher Self. Each has felt the warmth. Each has squeezed that hand and had that hand squeeze back. They knew they were experiencing more than a concept, more than a theory, because concepts and theories do not squeeze back! They knew they were not dealing with an attractive face of their negative ego, because they went through the middle steps. Subtly or overtly, we took them through these specific steps. As you go through them now, you too can know.

## *Letting Go of the Past*

The child within was never loved "good enough." It is time for you to meditatively love that child. It is time for you to go within and give that child the love that is missing. Whether the sense of missing love was real or imagined, give the child the love.

You see, time is an illusion. It exists as a convention of convenience. All time is simultaneous. The day you were born and the day you choose to die are right now. All your lifetimes are concurrent. There are those lifetimes that occur in the same space, but in a different time; they are called past lifetimes. Then there are the lifetimes that are in the same time, but in a different space; they are called parallel lifetimes. There really is no time, nor is there really any space. There is just the illusion of time and space, which is what you call the Physical Plane.

The child who wants love — the child who stubbornly refuses to grow until they get that missing love — is as alive today as they were "then." Many of you spend your whole life trying to appease that child.

There are those who continuously project parent onto everyone in their current life so that they can identify with the child they left behind so many years ago. Many men are drawn into relationships seeking a mother, not a wife or lover or friend. They find someone who will play the role of mother, and all is well — for a time. Even when they find a willing partner to dance the dance of mother-son, eventually they will realize that "try as you might, you are not my mother!" They will leave, looking for another player in their play. The dance continues.

If they cannot find a willing partner, or the previous player grows weary, it really does not matter. They will project mother anyway. In fact, they will project mother on everyone. Sex is no restriction. Bosses and friends become just as likely dance partners.

Men can also project fathers and siblings and any number of "ex's" — ex-wife, ex-boss, ex-lover, ex-friend — onto anyone. The past really has no limit. Well, except one: It is not now. Women not only project fathers, but mothers as well. The whole panoply is available if you want to live in the past — if you want to see the world through the eyes of "then."

The problem: Those eyes will never see satisfaction or victory. Those eyes will never see the way Home. Those eyes will never see the Sacred Journey.

There is also an adolescent within. The adolescent is usually in a state of sheer panic. When you were a child you thought you could remain a child forever, and the body betrayed you. Oh yes, many of you counted the days until the first signs of "growing up" appeared. Once puberty hit, you discovered that teen-age and adolescence were more than getting whiskers and developing breasts. There were hormones that you had not counted on. There were social pressures not expected. There was adulthood looming far too quickly on the horizon.

There is still an adolescent inside of you, an adolescent filled with panic, filled with terror. Many grown-up people are still adolescents in disguise. Many are still trying to finally "get it right."

If you insist upon replaying the past — if you insist upon trying to do it over and over until you get it right — until you are vindicated, then realize that the price is that you will not find the Sacred Journey.

Through the lens of your negative ego you want to relive it and make it right. The negative ego uses righteousness and blame or self-pity and self-importance to hold you in the past. It uses avoiding success to keep you clinging to the past.

There are techniques to find that child and adolescent within. There are meditations that can release the past and the hold it has on you, but you must want to let go. You must be willing not only to let go of the past, you must also be willing to turn to the future. You live in the now. We are not suggesting that you blind yourself with future hopes any more than we are encouraging you to be lost in the labyrinth of the past. No. Live in the now, but motivate yourself with the future.

Develop a Dream. Fill yourself with the desire, imagination and expectancy of what someday can be. Start looking at who you can become. Yes, admit how you have been. Recognize what you have done. Acknowledge that it was you who created that pain — that ugliness. Then forgive yourself and change. Let go of the past, and reach joyously for the future.

You have a basic choice. You can either wear the mask of the negative ego and live constantly trying to vindicate or rectify the past, or you can wear the mantle of your Future Self and live in the ever-present now, continuously creating more and more of who you can be.

Both avenues are available. One leads nowhere and is filled with the sadness of inevitability and the pain of loneliness. The other leads Home and is overflowing with the shimmer of possibility and the wonder of love.

## *Elegance*

Elegance means creating the maximum benefit with the minimum expenditure of energy. We are not speaking of it in the fashion sense. The person who seeks the Sacred Journey — the person who is already on its Path — functions with elegance.

There is a reality you want to create. With great angst, you have finally decided what it is you really want — well, sort of. You have decided, unless someone has a better idea. Well, you have decided, you tell yourself, still not fully convinced.

Now you program. You try to visualize, but you can't quite find that perfect relaxed position and your mind drifts and you fall asleep, but you meditated, sort of. . . . Then you worry.

You try to remember that you create it all. You try to remind yourself that programming really works. . . . Then you worry.

To be safe, you do three or four different meditations, all somewhat haphazardly. You go into self-pity hoping "someone up there" will take pity and do something. At this point you don't care if they like you or not — "just do something!"

Now it's time for your ritual of doubt and undeservability. Next will be attempts to manipulate the reality just in case you don't really create it.

You may or may not create the reality you requested. You will always create the reality you want — not always the one you ask for. Regardless of what is ultimately manifested — even if you create what you ask for — you did not do it with elegance.

Another approach: You decide what you want. You know what you want. You select the particular technique that somehow you know will work. Perhaps you select a series of techniques and design a strategy of reality creation.

Techniques accomplished, you easily stretch your success image, and you begin to act "as if" the reality were already yours. You begin to feel the gratitude and the joy.

The reality is yours. You accept it with celebration.

In both cases, the end result may well be the same. The means, however, vary drastically. At one time in your growth, all that was important was creating the success. In the midst of the Human Potential Movement and even the Metaphysical Potential Movement, many did not care how you created, just so you did create what you wanted.

On the Sacred Journey, you will, of course, create success. What really matters is how you create it. What really matters is the level of elegance with which your create the reality you both want and ask for.

When you function with elegance you use your metaphysics, and you do so smoothly. You use your metaphysics with a grace — with aplomb.

To achieve this elegance, start with desire. You must always start with desire. Then clarify that desire. Make it personal; make it yours. Too often you desire what you are supposed to desire. Even if what the consensus reality wants for you and what you want for yourself are the same, you must clarify the desire — make it yours. Have vision. Become a visionary. Be willing to see a future that lies beyond the limits of logic and reason. Be willing to hope and dream and wonder about a world that could be. Then develop impeccability. Be willing to focus like a laser beam. Despite the distraction the world and your negative ego wish to put in your path, be impeccable in thought — do not lose sight of your Dream — of your vision.

If you develop these four qualities — Desire, Clarity of Desire, Vision, and Impeccability — they will combine and create a synergy. They will combine and create a whole that is greater than the sum of the parts. They will create elegance.

Think of it. If you will honestly desire and not be timid about it, if you will make that *your* desire and not be shy about it, if you will have vision and hold it with the tenacity of impeccability, never losing grip on what you want, then of course you will create it with elegance!

Of course you will find yourself on the Sacred Journey.

## *Gratitude*

As a child you were taught to say "thank you" when it meant something and when it didn't. The words can tumble out of your mouth automatically. Therefore, you may assume feeling gratitude will be just as easy. Perhaps the word is as easy to say, but the feeling is more intricate to feel.  On your Sacred Journey, feeling gratitude can mean everything — just saying it, however, has no importance whatsoever.

What is gratitude?  Here is another concept defined in the metaphysical "you know" tradition.  Everyone knows the word, everyone knows it's important, but very few really know what it means.  We have spent hours exploring and unfolding the details and the subtlety of gratitude.  Its power still lies untouched.  Its depth is still unfathomed.

As part of your Sacred Journey, begin by realizing that gratitude is thankfulness.  It is thankfulness to those who have helped you create your own reality.  It is thankfulness to yourself and to your awareness, to your worth.  It is being thankful for the value you were willing to feel.  Gratitude is also being thankful that you were willing to create and willing to receive the love your seen and Unseen Friends continuously offer you.  Even if you were only willing to let it in for a moment, be grateful.

Gratitude is more than thankfulness.  It is also feeling joy.  Happiness is the fulfillment of your needs.  When you have a place that you can call your home and feel is your home, when you can work and be financially responsible, when you can engage your brain and mind in thinking about a future to unfold, then you are happy.

Joy is the fulfillment of your preferences.  Joy is the feeling of peace and tranquility that your home provides.  The productivity — the learning and understanding about yourself and about those with whom you interact while working — contains the joy in your career.  The joy is what turns a job into a career.  Joy is being able to dream Dreams that do not ever have to manifest.

For example, Isis Unlimited and Illuminarium Gallery are two galleries that our Peny owns.  The galleries are located on Rodeo Drive in Beverly Hills.  Visionary Publishing, Inc., another company that Peny created, is a very successful notecard and art book publishing company.  Many years ago Peny realized that it was important to create various businesses both as a creative outlet and so that Concept: Synergy could always be an endeavor or preference, a labor of love, and never a financial necessity.  We applaud her decision.  We want our work always to be a source of joy.  So it is.  It fulfills preferences, and therefore it is a joy.

Gratitude is feeling joyful.  Gratitude also involves spontaneity.  To be thankful, to be joyous is not enough.  To be spontaneously thankful and spontaneously filled with joy — that's gratitude.  If you have to think about it — if you have to remind yourself to feel it — you may be on the way, but you are not there yet.

Gratitude is a powerful tool.  If you will allow yourself to feel grateful, your processing and programming can work immeasurably better. Your success can be exponential. The "stuff" of life can improve markedly. As you feel grateful about what you have, you start having more things about which to feel that gratitude.

When you are using a reality creation technique that just does not seem to work, look at your level of gratitude. One of the major reasons people do not let the techniques work is that they do not want to feel grateful. There are many of you who will directly and indirectly sabotage yourselves just so you do not have to feel, or accidentally end up feeling, grateful.

Think about it. You have come across a particular reality-creation technique, and it works! Excitedly you use the technique, and eagerly you celebrate the ensuing successes. Then, strangely and without warning, you just stop. You forget to use the programming method. You just stop. This has happened to you many times. Often the reason has to do with guilt. You feel guilty because it's so easy. More often it is a reluctance to feel grateful.

It is amazing to watch people totally shut down successful realities just to avoid gratitude. Gratitude is powerful. If the resistance to or fear of it can shut down your entire reality, imagine what embracing it could do!

So why? Why are people afraid of gratitude? There are several reasons. Many are afraid of being used, feeling that if they are grateful then they are beholden, and therefore can be used. Others fear the hurt: They have felt thankful and have given away their power to the source of their gratitude only to be disappointed and hurt. They have silently decided, "Never again."

Still others fear appearing weak. They assume that "if I am grateful to you, then you have done something I did not or could not do for myself. You are stronger, I am weaker." Similarly, some are angry at the idea of gratitude; some hate feeling grateful. In fact, they do not really hate it. Gratitude makes some people feel needy. They do not hate gratitude: They hate needing.

Another resistance to gratitude results from the consequences of feeling it. When you feel grateful, it is really difficult also to blame and be righteous. It's impossible to feel self-pity. You just cannot be a victim, and martyrhood is impossible when you feel grateful.

You see, gratitude is a way of feeling love. You cannot feel love and self-pity at the same time. The two are mutually exclusive. However, when given a choice to feel self-pity or love, sadly, many will still choose self-pity. To them, gratitude is an enigma.

It is also very difficult to feel "better than" and to feel gratitude — though some have managed, with adroit mental gymnastics, to do so. Those of you who still want to be vindicated by reliving your past will not allow yourselves to feel grateful. Gratitude is an adult emotion that is felt spontaneously NOW.

Finally, many fear gratitude because it means there is something or someone "out there" who is more than them. Many want to think they are "all that is" because it is too frightening to consider that there just might be more out there than you know. Some go so far as to assert that they are the fullness and totality of God, just so they do not have to deal with the "something and someone more" who is out there.

When you feel grateful to a friend you are admitting that they are "more than you" — not "better than you" — just "more than you" at that spontaneous moment when they acted in such a way as to produce the bubbling up of gratitude in you. Many confuse "more than" with "better than." Perhaps that is because the consensus reality thinks that if some is good, more is better. The two are worlds apart.

The fear of "something more" increases when you feel grateful to your Unseen Friends — counsellors, guides, guardian angels, your Future Self, your Spiritual Self, your Soul, and your Higher Self. There are many Unseen Friends. Some say the spiritual path is a lonely path. Only if your path is one of hate and alienation is it lonely. If your path is filled with love, filled with the doingness from giving to caring so as to produce the beingness from security to knowing, then the spiritual path is crowded indeed! So many do not want to admit or deal with that unseen world. They run from gratitude because they do not want to admit or deal with a Love that just may be "more than" theirs.

We are a non-physical entity, a consciousness without form, a spark of light, a spark of love. We have never been physical. That is hard for people.

First, there is a certain egocentricity that says, "If I am physical, then everyone is." Certain people who live in California and in New York are shocked to hear that there is a world east of the Sierras and west of the East River. They are even more alarmed to realize that there are some of you who have no desire whatsoever to go to California or New York. They cannot believe that there are some people — there are those who actually exist — who have no intention of ever living in either place. It is startling!

Well, in similar fashion, there are those who have never been physical and have, likewise, no desire ever to do so. We are one.

Secondly, it is difficult because our existence says there is more out there than you know. There really is a "something and someone more" out there. The fact of our existence says there just might be a God/Goddess/All That Is out there, too.

"There just might be a God/Goddess/All That Is who loves me — who knows my name."

Not that we are that. No, but our existence makes the reality of God/Goddess/All That Is more possible — more real.

Those who fear or resist gratitude also find us difficult to accept. They find a living, breathing, loving, and embracing God/Goddess/All That Is even more difficult.

It would have been much easier, we suppose, to say that we once lived in Atlantis or Lemuria, or that we were a great monk somewhere high in the Himalayan Mountains. You could not verify that information, either. It would have been easier to make it so the Channel's body would walk around with eyes open. We suppose we could have just mimicked the Channel altogether and let everyone think we were him.

Any and all of these things would have made our message more digestible — would have made us more "appealing" to the consensus reality. The problem is that we have this quirky thing about honesty: We always insist upon it.

Also, part of why we are here is to remind you that there is a God/Goddess/All That Is who loves you and whom you love more than you have been willing to admit. Despite the hurt, you do love. Further, the reality of us reminds you about gratitude.

Both feeling gratitude and being grateful are integral parts of your Sacred Journey. Always remember: Gratitude is not a requirement of God/Goddess/ All That Is. Gratitude is a gift. It is a beautiful tool of your growth. It is a powerful force on your journey Home — on your Sacred Journey.

## *Aliveness*

Aliveness is a concept that is overlooked in your haste to grow. Your eagerness is encouraging, and sometimes you miss important nuances of growth. It is the nuances that give depth. It is the nuances that provide the richness and the sensuousness of evolution. You see, growth is not just about getting there. Everyone will make it — everyone will return Home. That is given. Growth is about the *way* you get there.

Aliveness, like elegance, more specifically deals with the "means" of your evolution. It deals directly with the quality of growth, not just the quantity.

Aliveness has four components. As you develop each, you will be more and more alive. You will be more and more vibrant.

THE FIRST IS LOVE.  As you work on loving yourself, then others, you have taken the first step of really being alive.

THE SECOND IS TRUST.  Trust is often a "throw-off" phrase.  When in doubt, tell them they need to trust themselves more, right?  Everyone needs more self-trust.  You cannot be wrong.  When you hear "trust yourself more," just like with "love yourself more," you shut down.  You stop listening.

Trust is one of the most powerful energies of creation you have available. Stop for a moment.  Think about your life and how it would change if, at the count of three, you totally trusted yourself.

One - two - three!  How much of your time is spent worrying, doubting, being confused?  How much energy do you throw away to anxiety?  How many defensive and manipulative moves could be eliminated?  Stop and really feel how your life could be — would be — different if only you trusted yourself more.  It is a powerful energy!

You are told a lot, but no one really teaches you *how*.  "Just do it, that's all.  Just start trusting."  Easier said than done.  Those who only tell you that have forgotten or are purposely ignoring the hurt.  You have tried to "just do it" before, and the pain is too much.

There are specific ways to learn to trust.  We will review them briefly. To begin, it is important to develop what we call the Synergy of Trust.  That is, do not rely only on one aspect of trust.  Rather, gather as much information as possible upon which to base your trust.  Listen to your body, but also listen to what your feelings say.  Do not stop there, however.  Tune into your mind. Listen to your intellect.  Then gather information from your intuition — pay attention to your hunches, or "gut level" responses.  As you gather information from all four parts of you, then combine what you know.  Out of this combination will come a synergy, an alchemy, of trust.

A decision about whether to take a certain job or not is haunting you. You just do not know what to do.  As you consider the pro's and con's, pay attention to the muscular and nerve responses of the body.  As you project what life will be like if you do or do not take the job, watch the emotions that bubble up.  With paper and pen list out all the advantages and considerations you have, but also hear your thinking.  Pay attention.  Finally, what is your "guess?"  What do your "guts" say?

Now, gather the data, not just from the list of pro's and con's, nor just from the advantages and considerations.  Do not gather the information only from your projected futures.  And do not listen only to your "guts."  As you cull the information from all seven avenues — pro's/con's, projections, advantages/considerations, body response, emotional response, mental response, and intuition — then the position of trust will emerge.

Another integral part of trust is knowing when to trust. Far too often you attempt to trust yourself when trust is not the issue at all. You try to trust yourself at times and in situations where trust does not apply. You fail. You feel anxious, which is what happens when you attempt to trust inappropriately. You decide you cannot trust.

Attempt trust only when it is appropriate. When is that?

There are four conditions that must be met to produce trust:

1) There must be a potential benefit and a potential harm.

2) Neither the benefit nor the harm has happened yet in your reality. One or the other will happen in the future.

3) The harm must be potentially more harmful than the benefit is beneficial.

4) You must truly and honestly expect the benefit.

These four conditions must be met. If any one of them is not, you do not have a situation of trust. If they do not exist, do not even attempt to trust. Forget it!

You buy a lottery ticket for one dollar and you could win millions! As part of your programming — as part of your techniques to create your success — you decide to really trust yourself. After all, you have heard that trust is a very powerful energy in conscious reality creation. Should you trust?

There is a benefit and a harm — you could win or lose. It is definitely in the future — the drawing is next month. However, the harm is not more harmful than the benefit is beneficial. If you lose, the harm is that you have lost one dollar. If you win, the benefit is that you win millions! The benefit is more beneficial than the harm is harmful. Do you really expect the benefit? Many would have to answer, "No, I never win contests," or "No, the odds are impossible," or "No, if I lose, it was just for fun. No."

This is not an issue of trust because the third condition was not met and fourth issue is dubious. Do not even attempt to trust yourself. You will fail. Even if you win the lottery, you will fail at trust. This is a situation of gambling, and you need to deal with it from that perspective.

Another example: You gain a friend's commitment to keep a secret, so you tell them some private information. If the information or fact that you told got back to the source, you would be in real trouble. Now that you have told, all you can do is trust. Is this a trust situation?

There is a benefit and a harm. They can keep the confidence or they can breach it. The potential benefit or harm is in the future. It may always be in the future. The harm is more harmful than the benefit is beneficial. If the confidence is breached, the harm is that all kinds of terrible things could happen. If the confidence is honored, the benefit is that life goes on as if nothing happened. You maintain the status quo. Nothing gets better — it just does not get worse. Finally, do you really expect the person to honor the confidence?

This is for you to answer honestly. This is definitely a situation of trust. All the criteria are met. Now you decide.

If you elicit a promise of confidence first, but secretly expect that the person will breach it, then it is not an issue of trust — it is an act of self-sabotage. If you tell them the confidence first and then, after the fact, attempt to elicit a promise "not to tell," then you are playing some sort of game — Russian Roulette, perhaps — but if you honestly expect them to honor the confidence, then it is still an issue of trust.

Do not set yourself up with trust. Create a synergy of trust, and then apply it where it is applicable.

Trust is a skill. Practice.

THE THIRD IS ENTHUSIASM. This is another misunderstood energy. You were enthusiastic as a child and were tolerated and eventually told to "grow up." You were warned of rude awakenings that would someday come. You were told of "comeuppances" that you would have: "You'll see . . . Mark my words!"

You lost your enthusiasm, dismissing it as the musings of a child or an adolescent. You gave up your enthusiasm to replace it with the yoke of being a grown-up — we will not say adult.

Now when you try to regain that lost treasure, you do not now how. Many will revert to childhood and to being a child, and then their enthusiasm only creates trouble. They withdraw.

This is an understandable reaction. Here you are in a grown-up world with grown-up intricacies and intimacies. You decide to be enthusiastic, and within minutes you are acting childish because that is the only reference point you have to enthusiasm. You start seeing the world through the mask — through the eyes — of the child.

All that intricacy and intimacy is frightening to a child. Working your job, driving your car, talking with your friends is fine for you, but from behind the mask of a child, through the eyes of a child, all those things are terrifying!

The child is going to mess up! The child does mess up. You retreat, abandoning enthusiasm.

Enthusiasm is not being childish and silly. Enthusiasm is not being manic. Enthusiasm is the synergy — the whole that is greater than the sum of the parts — of the free child, the curious adolescent, the nurturing parent, and the Future Self. Enthusiasm includes your relationship with your Higher Self.

Just as there is an adaptive child who wants the love they think they were denied, so there is a free child. You remember that free child. That's the part of you who could get lost in your coloring book. That's the part that could see a movie and play the leading roles for days. That's the part that could step outside of time and space. That's the part that could fly!

There is the panicky adolescent, but there is also the curious teen who wants to understand everything and is intrigued by everything as well. There is that teenager in you who could delve into projects with a poignant intimacy and intricacy that can bring tears to your eyes. That's the part of you who could be invisible just by thinking it so!

You are fully aware of the critical parent with all the should's and should not's. In the quiet time you can also know that nurturing parent who is sincerely concerned about doing it right. For many, that nurturing parent may be Mom or Dad. For others it may be a teacher, a sibling, a coach, or a special older friend. For each there was someone who cared. Whoever that was, they obviously cared enough because you are here. If you are reading this book, they maybe didn't care as much as you wanted, but they cared enough. Studies have shown that when children are truly deprived of adequate nurturing, they end up in institutions. You are here; you got enough.

All time is simultaneous. Just as the past is ever-present, so is the future. Just as you can meditatively go back in time to take care of the child within, so you have a Future Self who can take care of you. You have as many potential futures as you can imagine. Some are more likely than others. One is the best — the optimum future for you. You can call upon that Future Self. You can allow that Future Self to help you become more of who you are and more of who you can be.

Part of the synergy of enthusiasm can be you and your Higher Self. That is what you are reaching for and seeking.

Allow these parts of you — the Free Child, the Curious Adolescent, the Nurturing Parent, and the Future Self — to work together. Draw upon their energy, their love. When you start looking at your present and your future through their collective eyes, you will know enthusiasm and the power of aliveness that it brings.

THE SACRED JOURNEY  82

THE FOURTH IS EXPECTANCY.  In your world today you are told to lower your expectations.  You are told you will just be disappointed and hurt if you expect things to be great.  "Tighten your belt.  Lower your expectations.  Then when you are disappointed, it won't hurt so much."

When it hurts just as much, you decide you should have lowered your expectations even more.  Lowered expectations are not an anaesthetic.  They never have been.  When there was hope of success, you proclaimed loud and clear how you had no anticipation at all!  "Honest, I don't really care . . . honest."  Then when the loss came, it still knocked the wind out of you.  It still hurt.  You tell yourself it would have hurt more.  It would not have, and a part of you knows we are telling the truth.

Part of how you create your reality is by expecting it to be wonderful.  When you lower those expectations, you diminish your ability to create "the win."  The very act of lowering your anticipation to protect you from the pain is exactly what is producing the pain.

Lowered expectations never eliminate the raw sting of failure.  Raised expectations, however, provide the missing ingredient that ultimately secures the celebration of success.  Always enthusiastically expect the best!

If that enthusiastic anticipation does not secure the success, it will prepare you — it will provide greater strength — to handle what disappointment there is.  The failure will sting, but surprisingly less.

There is an important distinction here.  We are talking about high expectations, not flights of fancy.  We are talking of adult Dreams, not adolescent fantasies.

Expectations are born in the realm of possibility. The possible becomes probable through the mysterious alchemy of trusting love and enthusiastic expectation.  The probable becomes actual through the willingness to receive.

The Sacred Journey becomes more real with Aliveness.

## Active Resources:  Sharpened Tools

The last of the middle steps is to take inventory of the resources out of which you create your reality.  Then review and sharpen the specific tools of creation.

You create your reality out of choices and decisions, thoughts and feelings, and attitudes and beliefs.  That is all.  There are no other raw materials — no other resources — that you, or anyone else, use.  Those who are creating more exciting realities than you are doing so out of the same "stuff."

Your thoughts and feelings are propelled by your choices and decisions and compelled by your attitudes and beliefs into manifestation on the loom of desire, imagination, and expectancy.

Let's take that apart.

Your reality is the product of your thoughts and feelings. Some say just thoughts, others say just feelings create your reality. However, both work together to become your manifestations. To those of you who have learned only to trust your heart, try feeling without thinking. No matter what you try to feel, you need to create pictures, or sounds, or fields of resonance. That requires thought. You just cannot feel without thinking. Those who tell you to "just flow with it, just follow your heart, don't think, just feel" may make you feel guilty for being so crass as to think, but even though they won't admit it, they are thinking, too.

Similarly, you cannot just think without feeling. The two, despite the popular jargon, work together. Your reality has been referred to as frozen thought. We would suggest that it's frozen thought and feeling. More correctly: Your reality is the synergistic manifestation of what you think and what you feel.

The synergy aspect is important here. You see, you have all kinds of thoughts and a whole range of feelings. They all blend together, but the totality is not a product of arithmetic. The totality is exponential. You do not just add up all your thoughts and all your feelings and see what you come up with, and see what the total is. The thoughts and feelings combine and compound and double back on each other so that the result is this wondrously mysterious thing you call "your life." What propels what you think and feel? Choices and decisions.

The choices you make and the short- and long-term decisions that you create out of those choices propel your thoughts and feeling into manifestation. To be able to choose is one of the mystical gifts of being human. Other animals can choose, but their choices are based on instinct (unconscious mind activity) and habit (subconscious mind activity). Human animals have that same level of choice. Then, remember, something happens and you realize that there is more to life than just surviving. You make the first choice of growth, and your evolution begins. That choice propelled the thoughts and feelings you had been having all along. That choice propelled them into action. The action is called evolution — growth.

You are making choices all the time. That you pretend you are unconscious does not make it so. Even to choose not to choose is a choice. To take no action is a choice.

Once you choose, a decision is born. A choice, dynamically manifest, first shows up as a decision.

Your thoughts and feelings are not only propelled, they are compelled into synergistic manifestation. Your attitudes and beliefs compel what you think and feel into the density you call physicality. In fact, all the thoughts you have and the feelings you feel spring forth from the well of attitude and belief. To think it or to feel it — whatever "it" is — you must first hold it as an attitude and belief.

Where do your thoughts come from? What is the origin of your feelings? The question is profound; the answer, disarming. They both come from the same place — your attitudes and beliefs. Where your attitudes and beliefs come from is a whole different issue. We will look at that with you some day.

Belief precedes reality. Your intellect can accept that. However, until you own it on an emotional level, until you own it in every cell of your body, until it becomes a part of your breath, metaphysics and spirituality will only be a theory to you. Yes, we mean that. It may be a fascinating theory. It may even be a theory that works some of the time or even a great deal of the time, but it will still be a theory. It will not really be a way of life. When you do own this — belief does precede reality — then you open yourself to whole new "set" of reality. You discover a metaphysics and a spirituality that hitherto only existed in your "wouldn't it be wonderful if . . ."

There are many, many people involved in metaphysics — some who even call themselves leaders — who do not (nor intend to) ever really understand the core: "I create my own reality." They never intend to really own that belief precedes reality, that belief precedes the illusion you create called reality. They will be very surprised when you do own it. They will be very chagrinned when you move on to the new "set." They will not understand the visions you have and the vista you will realize. You will not understand what they are waiting for.

Don't wait!

What happens when you hold a certain belief? Here is an example using the belief "love hurts."

Love hurts. This is a basic belief that many of you hold. First you create the belief, and then you proceed to create the reality to prove it. Love hurts. This belief colors your lens to the world. It produces your attitude. With this attitude, through this lens, you will see the world in a unique way.

Love hurts. The belief, and the attitude it spawns, form the well from which spring your thoughts and feelings. What thoughts would you expect to come from this well? What feelings?

Love hurts. The thoughts and feelings synergistically manifest into physical form. What kind of friendships do you expect? Think about the level and the intensity of giving, responding, respecting, and knowing you would offer when love hurts. What security, pleasure, vulnerability, and trust would you provide?

Love hurts. Out of the attitude and belief spring the thoughts and feelings. Out of the thoughts and feelings the choices and decisions are formed.

Thoughts and feelings are propelled by choices and decisions and compelled by attitudes and beliefs into manifestation on the loom of desire, imagination, and expectation. You will create relationships in which love hurts.

Here is another example using the belief "love heals."

Love heals. This belief will produce a certain coloring, too. "Love heals" will generate its own unique attitudes.

Love heals. Quite different thoughts and feelings will spring from the wells of attitude and belief. There will be anticipatory thoughts and feelings of aliveness. There will be thoughts of love and light and laughter and joy. There will be feelings of gratitude.

Love heals. The thoughts and feelings will form powerful choices and decisions that stretch and reach into the future. There will be choices of intimacy and commitment. There will be the decisions to love.

Love heals. Healthy relationships will be created. Love will grow. You will grow. . . . Love heals!

Belief precedes reality. You create your own reality. There is no fine print.

Inventory your resources, your raw materials. However, do more than that: Recognize, acknowledge, forgive yourself and change those raw materials that are hurting you and others. Also, recognize, acknowledge, congratulate yourself, and continue those choices and those beliefs that are working and that are healing you, others, and your world.

As well as having resources out of which to create your reality, you have tools — specific tools — with which to shape, carve, and sculpt your personal reality.

Desire, imagination, and expectancy are the tools of reality creation. No one has more, no one has less.  Those you envy are using the same tools to create their reality as you are using to create yours.

Where do you get these tools?  From Dreaming.  From daydreams to night dreams, from altered states to the worlds that exist when you meditate, that is where the tools are born, from the larger Dream — the conscious personal and global Dream of the future.  The tools come from your Vision. All Dreams use desire, imagination, and expectation, and they replenish the supply and always add to it.

The steps of getting there are the qualities of being there.  What it takes to Dream is what Dreaming gives back exponentially.

It is like a perpetual motion machine.  The more you desire, imagine, and expect, the more desire, imagination, and expectancy you will have.  No one gives it to you.  No one can take it away.

The last of the middle steps is to remind yourself of your resources. Keep them active.  Many of you have learned of the resources before.  We have mentioned them many times before.  But, you see, the Sacred Journey involves more than memory and lists.  It involves not just knowing the truths — it involves living them.  Therefore, keep the resources active.

On your Sacred Journey it is important to sharpen your tools regularly.  It is important to Dream in as many ways as you can.  It is important to Dream. It is important to have Vision.  Vision is a Dream that involves all five of the senses.  You dream the Dream so vividly that you can see it — at least see it with your heart.  You can hear it, smell it, touch it.  You can even taste it. When a dream becomes that much a part of you, then it becomes a Vision.

On the Sacred Journey it is important to continuously activate the resources and sharpen the tools.  It is important to have a personal and a global Vision.

You are well on your way.  The culminating step is next.  Welcome . . .

# Five

## The Journey Home:

### Communion with Your Higher Self

To begin your Sacred Journey, the first step is love. It is important to remember the obvious reasons to love and then to understand the not-so-obvious reasons to love. Properly motivated, you learn the skill and the art of loving first yourself, then others, and then your world. With a solid foundation, your journey has begun.

With the momentum of love, you then let go of the past. You release the child and adolescent. You stop the games you play with the real or imagined parents. You release the past, not because you are bad and wrong, but because reaching for the future is so much more productive — so much more fun. The thought of having a living, breathing, loving, embracing relationship with your Higher Self on your way Home to God/Goddess/All That Is is far more exciting — far more tantalizing — then the same old merry-go-round of the past. You are motivated out of anticipation and expectation, not out of shame.

Having released the past, you turn to the future fully aware that you live in the now. You develop elegance, gratitude, and aliveness. The excitement increases. You begin to see your way home! Uncertain as to where you were going and how you would get there, you now catch a glimpse, albeit brief, of what this journey is all about. It really is about you and your Higher Self. It really is about you and a God/Goddess/All That Is who really loves you. It really is.

The energy builds as you recharge, retune, and retone yourself by inventorying your raw materials. You not only take inventory, you evaluate and change the choices and decisions that are counterproductive. You realign the thoughts and feelings so they are more consistent with who you are becoming rather than with who you were pretending to be. You explore, and when appropriate, you change the attitudes and beliefs. With raw materials ready, you sharpen the tools of creation. You are now ready for the culminating step to fully begin your journey. You are now ready to discover your Higher Self.

## *The Last Step is Last*

The culminating step to begin your Sacred Journey is last for a reason. Before you can discover your Higher Self, you have to decide if there really is a Higher Self to be discovered. No one can decide for you. You must do it on your own. To make that decision honestly, it is important that you prepare yourself by "taking" the first six steps first, and then by "taking" this last step last.

We encourage you to take the beginning and the middle steps in the order suggested so you can more powerfully, more responsibly, complete your preparation. Once that preparation is complete and you know you are honestly ready for the Sacred Journey, with a smile you will realize you are already on it! Truly, the steps of getting there are the qualities of being there!

Many can take you on meditations. Many can tell you that you should meet your Higher Self. Touching and moving pictures can seductively stimulate desire. However, without the proper preparation you are left with the haunting questions: "Did I really get in touch with my Higher Self? . . . Was it real?"

Occasionally it just might be real — maybe you "lucked out." Most often, as you well know, it was not real. After a few thrilling meditations, your fervor dims. The information, the help so eagerly anticipated, creates more struggle and strife, not less. You lose interest. You stop.

Hopefully that is all you do. Many blame themselves and conclude that they are failures. Everyone else, they assume, is doing just fine. Many stuff the feelings of failure; they punish themselves and resent others. More than just stop, they get hurt and they hurt others. More than being hurt and hurting, they give up on ever having a relationship with their Higher Self. Some give up on ever growing. The pain could have been avoided if you had loved yourself enough to be patient. The hurt and hurting never would have happened if you had taken each step in turn as you prepared to meet your Higher Self. But no one told you there were steps. They just said, "Do it!"

There is no value in blaming them. Perhaps they naïvely did not know there were steps, either. Maybe they did have ulterior motives and a negative ego that ran amuck. Maybe you did, too.

There is no value in blaming. Forgive yourself. The point is you do know there are steps now. Use what you know now.

We have a reputation not only for providing a vast range of techniques for any situation that may arise in your reality, but also for providing techniques that are uncanny because *they work!*

Of course, no one can guarantee any technique. You are the one who decides whether this technique, that meditation, or even that ritual will really work for you. This fact can be a tremendous insight on your part, or a clever cop-out on the part of those offering shallow techniques.

No matter how effective or ineffective the method, it will not work until you are willing. When people are not willing and the approach, therefore, does not work, so often they either punish themselves as failures or walk away from metaphysics calling it the failure. Instead, we would advise them to review the technique to see if it is valid and then to review their own willingness to succeed. No punishment or abandonment is necessary.

Some, who are quick to offer techniques and meditations to solve this problem or that, rely on this willingness issue to cover the fact that their methods are ineffective. The approach they suggest does not really work. Upon the rare occasion that it has worked (much to their surprise), the success belongs to the power of willingness, not to the effectiveness of the technique.

The bottom-line truth is that any technique will work when you are ready to change. However, when you finally are ready — really ready — why not have really effective and powerful techniques lined up and ready to use? It is so sad to see people get themselves into a mind set where they are willing to jump — ready to change — and then are saddled with ineffective techniques. They can still make it, but there are much more elegant ways!

The reason the techniques we offer are so effective is not really such a mystery. They work because we not only give you techniques, we offer you the preparation that allows them to work in your reality. We love you. We care. We are committed to your growth. We prepare you and teach you because we do love you.

If you will start at the beginning and gracefully and gently take each step — take the steps one at a time — when you are ready to succeed, you will.

## *The Last Step You Take Alone*

To take this final step of preparation, it is important that you answer certain questions for yourself.  No one else can effectively answer them for you.

The first question:  Is there really a Higher Self to even bother discovering?  Obviously, if the Higher Self is some New Age or metaphysical hype — some PR stunt — then no technique will work and everyone might as well just "pack it in," as they say.

Then it is essential that you have an appreciation of — that you understand the personal value of — connecting with your Higher Self.  So many assume they understand, but few actually do see the value without some introspection.  You have heard that it is valuable for so long, there have been so many workshops and seminars about your Higher Self, that naturally you assume you know just how important it is.  And ultimately you are right that it is.  However, you have to come to that conclusion for yourself.  You have to come to that conclusion on your own.  No one can make that decision for you.

Thirdly, it is helpful to understand the topography, the "lay of the land" as it were.  It is important to grasp the relationship and the relative placement of the higher aspects of yourself — including Higher Self, Future Self, and Soul — with the inner aspects of yourself — including Conscious, Subconscious, and Unconscious Selves.  This relationship needs to be real for you.  We can show you a diagram, but the relationship and relative positioning has to be yours.  No one can do it for you.

Finally, to complete your preparation for the Sacred Journey, it is valuable to consider the meaning of three words: communication, union, and communion.  The last is the relationship you seek with your Higher Self as your companion on this most beautiful and special Journey Home.  Again, you must come to peace with communion with your Higher Self on your own.

If it is not eminently clear, the final step of preparation is taken alone.  Whereas there are specific techniques and precise steps to take as you encounter the first six steps, with this final step you have to step out on your own — there are no specific techniques and no precise steps to take.

You must be like the Fool of the Tarot, standing on the brink.  And like a Fool, you must step off the edge . . . alone.

In nature, God/Goddess/All That Is provides perfect balance and perfect grace.  As the final step must be taken alone, and therefore may appear to be the most difficult, God/Goddess/All That Is provides extra help.

First, by the time you get to the seventh and last step, having completed the first six successfully, you are more prepared and readier than ever to make the choices and decisions necessary to move forward elegantly.

Additionally, a wonderful synergy occurs by the time you have reached this seventh step, a wonderful synergy that easily propels and compels you. The last step, the most difficult if you attempt it without preparation, will be the easiest once you are ready — really ready — to take it.

Synergy is defined as when the whole is greater than the sum of the parts. An example: You have an aluminum cylinder that is closed at one end and has a clear screw-on cap, two D-type batteries, a tiny bulb, a spring, and a little switch. When you just add up all the parts randomly you have "junk." When you combine the parts in a particular and unique way, you create a flashlight and not only that, you have created light. The whole — light — is much greater than the sum of its parts. Synergy.

When you have completed the first six steps of preparation, you have much more than a lot of notes and a lot of theory and philosophy, which, on their own, would be considered by many to be "junk." You have created "light." You have created the "light" to see your way home. You have created the "light" to be able to "see" your Higher Self. You have created the "light" to be able to reach out and touch — to reach out and be touched by — that Higher Self who has been waiting, who has been waiting all the time, waiting just for you.

Let's begin. Let's finish.

## *Is There Really A Higher Self?*

Though you must answer this question for yourself and by yourself, we can offer some pointers. We can give you a few clues.

There is no scientific proof that you have a Higher Self. For that matter, there is no empirical evidence that conclusively demonstrates a Subconscious or an Unconscious Self, either.

Yes, research has shown that your body weight does change between the fully conscious state and the deep sleep state. Many have taken this as proof that these other Selves exist. In fact, it really does not prove this at all. Some say that when you sleep your consciousness leaves the body, and that the loss in weight, albeit minimal, proves it.

It demonstrates some shift, but what exactly leaves your body? Does your conscious mind leave, or is it your Subconsciousness or your

Unconsciousness that leaves?  Does anything come into your body while you sleep?  Maybe when you sleep all your internal organs "lighten up!"

Some have said that it is your Soul that leaves, and therefore they erroneously say your Soul weighs a certain definitive amount!

In fact, the shift in consciousness that travels through the fourth ventricle of the brain is measurable as you go into and come out of deep states of meditation or certain levels of sleep.  This shift, however, does not prove the existence of the Subconscious, Unconscious, or the Soul.

There is no proof.  There is no proof of the Higher Self.

There was a land that was called Atlantis.  It was located in the midst of the vast Atlantic.  Civilizations rose and fell.  Due to the corruption, the misuse of power, and the disrespect for nature, the land once called Atlantis destroyed itself.  It "sank into the ocean."  The great land called Atlantis will rise again.

There are those who have taken pictures of the shallows off Bimini and other Caribbean Islands and claim to have definitive proof that Atlantis really was.  Their photographs show what they claim are walls and roadways and remnants of buildings.  The angles, they say, are too defined to be anything else but manmade.  They are too sophisticated, they add, to have been constructed by anything less than an advanced society that once was.

There are others who contend just as conclusively that the story of Atlantis is merely a myth created to illustrate the importance of respecting nature, of using power correctly, and of not being corrupt.  The critics say that the Egyptians wrote down a legend telling of a small volcanic island in the Mediterranean Sea that exploded and was destroyed (this is geological fact) and that then they created a myth to teach their children.  The Greeks and Romans — believing everything they read — took the myth as fact.  Thus was born the "fact" of Atlantis.

Who is correct?  To date, neither group can prove themselves correct.

There was a land called Lemuria.  It was before Atlantis, existing in the mists of the Pacific.  Though cloaked in mist it was a land of luminescence.  Though your egocentricity cannot assume anything can disappear without being destroyed, Lemuria was not attacked by Atlantis, nor by any other civilization. Lemuria finished. Lemuria was done. Lemuria disappeared back into the mist from whence it came.

Do not get out your glass-bottomed boats.  You will find no evidence of Lemuria.  There will be no proof.

On the leading edge of physics are a number of courageous and daring people who are exploring the farthest reaches of the Quantum.  In their search and research, they are demonstrating on blackboards and computer screens the basic tenets of metaphysics. They are proving that each of you is creating your own reality. More than speculating, they are demonstrating that reality is the creation of observed consciousness. They are showing the world that all of your universe — and universes — exists as a product of thought and feeling.

Some say they are starting to see the face or faces of God show through. Science can demonstrate that if any of the forces — strong force, weak force, gravity, and electromagnetic force — were any different, even by the smallest amount, a tiny bit more or a minute bit less, your world would not exist. There are too many exacting measurements to be explained by random chance, they say. Perhaps they are about to prove God!

God/Goddess/All That Is will not be caught — will not be imprisoned — in the dust of blackboard chalk or in a grid of 80 or 132 columns and 66 lines. The day science "proves" God is the day you lose God. God/Goddess/All That Is will never be proved.

## The Story of Two Bridges

There are two bridges that you can cross. One is called the Bridge of Faith, and the other is called the Bridge of Belief.

The Bridge of Faith is long and flat. It goes on for what must seem like forever. As you stand at the beginning of the Bridge of Faith, it's like looking down a railroad track in Kansas. It goes on forever until the parallel tracks appear to meet. With the railroad track, however, you know they don't really meet. The Bridge of Faith looks the same way except that eventually the two sides do meet, because the Bridge of Faith goes on to the end of time — or more precisely, it goes on until it is beyond time. Time and Space are illusions which together comprise the fourth dimension of your illusory reality. In outer space, when Time and Space collapse, when they end, you call it a Black Hole. This is where all Time, all Space, all Light collapse.

The Bridge of Faith also collapses into a single point in time/space and disappears. There is no end to the Bridge of Faith.

Those involved in Traditional Spirituality are crossing the Bridge of Faith. To Eastern faiths, the bridge is the one they cross between the many lives of karma. For them the traffic is two-way and seldom ending. To the Jewish faith The Bridge of Faith is the bridge from pain to the Promised Land, from being lost to being found, from being without their King to finding the Messiah. To some of the Christian faith, the Bridge of Faith is short — it only goes from here to the Second Coming, which could be any day now. And for others it is forever!

The other bridge is called the Bridge of Belief. It is quite different. It is arched very steeply, though it is easy to cross if you know how. The arch is so steep that you cannot see over the crest of the arch until you get there. Once you do get there, it is rumored, then you can see clearly all that lies on the other side. No one who has not crossed the Bridge of Belief, however, can substantiate this claim of clarity. No one can say whether the claims, the rumors, are true or not. Those who have crossed it say it is true, but no one can prove it. They cannot prove it, because what they claimed to have experienced was beyond words, and what they saw was slightly different for each of them. There is no chance for empiricism there. There is no proof!

There is also something very strange about the Bridge of Belief. Once someone begins crossing, it can be an ordeal where one has to be a warrior attempting to conquer the obstacles along the way. However, the crossing also can be an adventure filled with wonder and with exciting encounters. The difference seems to be in the preparation and the desire, the imagination, and the expectancy.

Something else: When someone is crossing, everyone else can watch just like with the Bridge of Faith. However, when they reach that crest over which no one can see, they have a choice: Go on or go back. If they choose to go on, they also disappear out of view. Very strange, this Bridge of Belief.

Those of you who have known, or at least now know, what the New Spirituality, the New Age, is really all about, are the ones involved with the Bridge of Belief. You see, those of you crossing the Bridge of Belief and those crossing the Bridge of Faith are really looking for the same thing. You are all looking for God/Goddess/All That Is, by whatever name you use.

## *Beyond the Bridge of Belief*

What lies beyond the Bridge of Belief? You will have to cross the bridge to fully see, but let us tell you this. Beyond the Bridge of Belief lie Atlantis and Lemuria. Beyond of Bridge of Belief is where you will find your Higher Self and your Soul. Beyond the Bridge of Belief is God/Goddess/All That Is.

Nothing that lies beyond this bridge can ever be empirically — scientifically — proved. If it could be, it would no longer exist . . . beyond the Bridge of Belief! Once you get to the crest, and not before, you will see what we mean. It is beyond words in its wonder, and it is beyond words because language is linear and the reality that is beyond is non-linear.

Once you reach the crest, and not before, you will change. You will step out of one Set of reality constraints, and you will step into another freer, more powerful, and more responsible Set. Your world will never be the same again.

There is no need for fear. You do not have to abandon anything you have already had, but it will never quite be the same once you cross the Bridge.

Some have crossed back, forgetting what they knew, forgetting what they understood. They pretend everything is as before. They even re-create all their old problems, obstacles, and blockages. They gather up all their old raw materials from the choices they used to make to the beliefs they used to have. It is very difficult. Once you have crossed the Bridge of Belief, it is much more difficult to fail than it is to succeed! To fail you have to keep remembering the lie!

For all intents and purposes, they are their same old self. But underneath — very deep — they know. They know what lies beyond proof. They know there is a God/Goddess/All That Is! No, they did not see All That Is on the other side of that Bridge, but within each cell of their body, they knew and still know: "There is a God/Goddess/All That Is who loves me . . . and whom I love!"

Your Higher Self exists beyond the Bridge of Belief. You see, we know this, because in your reality, we lie beyond the Bridge of Belief, too.

You must decide on your own whether or not there is a Higher Self. Cross the bridge. . . . You are ready. . . . Cross the Bridge of Belief.

## *Importance of Connecting with your Higher Self*

In your search for Truth you will hear of the concept of your Higher Self. As a concept it may have many different names. It is up to you to decide whether the concept is real or not. It is up to you to decide whether the Higher Self is a philosophy worth learning like so many other philosophies, or whether, when you reach out and touch your Higher Self, it will reach back — whether it will touch you. You have to decide if the Higher Self is going to be a figment of your mental gyrations, or whether when you squeeze its hand, it will squeeze back.

This decision, though essential, is not enough. As well as accepting the reality of your Higher Self, you need to understand the importance of connecting with it. You need to comprehend why it is so valuable, especially now, to make contact, and more, to connect with that aspect of who you are and who you are becoming.

The importance of connecting has to be your importance, not ours. We can point out some potential reasons, but they must make sense to you — not us. The relevance must be real to you — not us.

What we are saying sounds so obvious that we know many of you will skim over these words wanting to get on to the "important stuff." This is the important stuff.

Yes, we are going to lay out techniques in the form of meditations. We are going to suggest specific, step-by-step ways of working with your Higher Self that will have definite and precise impact upon your current reality and the future reality you are creating.

Those things are important. You can follow the meditations and work with the techniques, and you can create a very workable, very valuable, relationship with your Higher Self. After all, there are no limitations.

We will never tell you that if you do not "do it" the way we say, you will not succeed. We will never say that because that is a lie. Our techniques are uncanny because they work so well, but they are not the only methods that will work. You can create your own techniques, for that matter, that can produce a very workable Higher Self relationship.

What we are saying is that if you will follow the steps with precision, you can not only create a valuable relationship, you can also develop a connection with your Higher Self that you know is real — really real, not just theoretically real.

Also you can have a depth, a richness, to that relationship that, at first, you will think is "too good to be true." Shortly thereafter, however, when the richness and depth grow, you will come to realize that there is nothing that is too good to be true. There are only things "good enough to be true!"

So, make the importance — make the value — of connecting with your Higher Self something that means a great deal to you. Perhaps use some of the suggested reasons as catalysts to develop your own very private and very personal reasons.

## *Reasons to Consider*

*One:* Metaphysics is growing up. The carnival atmosphere that the lack of discernment has allowed is slowly coming to an end. More and more metaphysics will be called upon to provide real solutions to real issues. The "you need to trust yourself . . . the space brethren will swoop down and rescue us" type of answers will be less prevalent. Real answers will start emerging.

These real answers will come from a living relationship with a Higher Self who can work with you to create a more vibrantly successful reality.

*Two:* The world is filled with solutionless problems. More and more you are aware that as one solution is proposed, it tends to create ten more problems. Your reality is trying to tell you that "the old paradigm is not working . . . the usual logic-base, cause-effect scenario just no longer applies . . . The old ways are not working." Your reality is trying to tell you: "Stop trying to clean the old floor. Start creating new floors. . . . Stop trying to make the old Set work. Start creating new Sets." Linear logic needs to be replaced with exponential visionary thinking.

Well, the words sound nice, but how do you do that!? This is where a loving relationship with your Higher Self can make the difference.

The beauty of the higher realms is that they are in perfect harmony. As the problems get more difficult, as the solutions, which are there, require more sophistication, there is a greater level of power — a greater level of help — available. Though the Higher Self has always been there, it has never been so necessary and subsequently so available. Please hear this: Though the Higher Self has always been there, it has never, in the history of humankind, been so necessarily a part of the solution, and subsequently it has never been as available as it is now, and it has never been as easy to make contact.

*Three:* The New Age is really new! More and more you are consciously creating your own reality! In fact, you are totally creating your reality from conscious thought. You are still pretending those thoughts are coming from some dark recesses of a mind and brain you do not — and say you cannot — understand. As you accept the truth, it can become frightening. You can feel all alone — lonely. After all, you are discovering that you create it all. You are realizing that everything and everyone is subject to your creation — to your Dream.

Panicking, some turn away, pretending it's not true. Fearing, some withdraw to avoid the responsibility implied. Numbing, others close down their thoughts and feelings as best they can. Reaching, many of you turn inward searching for a friend. You have a friend in your Higher Self. In fact, you are never alone. You never have to feel lonely. You may need someone to turn to. If you need a friend, your Higher Self is there.

*Four:* There is too much to know. Once, a long time ago, it was possible for one person to know it all. Jefferson? Franklin? Though one can argue as to who did and who did not know all that there was to know, everyone can agree that, with the proliferation of knowledge in the last several decades, there is no one now who knows everything. Not only is it impossible to know everything that there is to know in the world, it's even impossible to know everything "just you" need to know to live your life fully and happily.

You need help. Science and technology offer the computer. Spirituality offers your Higher Self. In your world, there is room for both!

*Five:* You deserve. So often you are taught that you have to do your growth on your own. "Growth is a lonely path," remember? There are often choices and decisions you must make on your own. This last step of preparation for the Sacred Journey is enhanced by making the appropriate decisions on your own. It adds a depth and a richness — it adds a realness — to the loving relationship you are about to have with your Higher Self. Making the choices and decisions on your own adds a realness that otherwise just might not be there.

Choices and decisions may be made on your own, but growth does not have to be alone or lonely. You can have help. You deserve help. God/Goddess/All That Is never intended that life should be filled with struggle and strife. They never intended that you should feel pain. The Physical Plane was intended to be a celebration of exploration and a celebration of being alive.

You and your negative ego said the pain was valuable. You made that decision, not God/Goddess/All That Is! Connect with your Higher Self because you deserve it! You deserve it, not because you earned it — you deserve it just because you are!

Just because . . . you are.

*Six:* Spirituality is real. We know that many who are involved actively or passively in Fundamentalist or traditional spirituality are there because of fear. They are taught as much. It is written, and in case you missed it, it is spoken: "Fear God!" Also, "Fear the Devil!" Yet others are involved because it is socially, economically, and politically wise. Either type of involvement is not based on faith — it is based on fear or pragmatism, but not on faith.

There is, however, yet a third group of Fundamentalists and traditionalists who are pursuing their spirituality actively or passively not out of fear or pragmatism, but out of sincere faith. There is this group of people who are traveling the Bridge of Faith. These are the ones who know spirituality is real. Whether you agree with the path they have chosen, at least they have chosen it because spirituality is real.

Within the new spirituality, within the New Age, there are many involved because it is chic. Some are involved as an act of rebellion: "Exactly how shocked will my family be?"

Further, there are those who see the social, economic, and political potential of the New Age. More recently, due to all the "doom and gloom" talk, there are those who are also seduced by fear.

There is yet another group involved in the New Age. There are those who have begun to cross the Bridge of Belief. You — you are crossing this Bridge — you know spirituality is real. You know there is a God/Goddess/All That Is who really loves you — who knows your name. Also, you are just beginning to accept that you love that very real God/Goddess/All That Is, too!

As you wake up, as you really wake up to the realness of metaphysics and the realness of spirituality, you will want to connect with your Higher Self. You will want to connect because of that realness. "Because spirituality is real, I want my Higher Self."

Sadly, there are many still asleep. To them, metaphysics is a game, and spirituality is a buzz word. Happily, more and more will begin to wake up now. Your Higher Self will be waiting. . . .

*Seven:* You are growing up. You knew there was *something more.* You stepped outside of the consensus reality to begin looking for that *something more.* It may have taken you twenty, thirty, maybe fifty thousand years, but you are on the brink of finding it. Not only is metaphysics growing up, so are you.

You are a lot smarter than the bandwagoneers thought you were. You are able to discern, and you are beginning to discern. You are worth more than they thought, and you are beginning to really discover and accept your worth. You are powerful, and you are starting to take back that power more beautifully than ever before.

You are growing up, and your Higher Self is a critical part of that growth. You are discovering God/Goddess/All That Is, and your relationship with your Higher Self is an integral aspect of that new love . . . or is it LOVE?

Reasons why . . . you have to decide on your own. Decide!

## *The Topography of Consciousness*

Conscious, Subconscious, Unconscious, and Higher Conscious Minds . . . Past, Present, and Future Selves . . . Higher Self (is that different than Higher Consciousness . . . is it the same?) . . . Soul, Spirit, God, God/Goddess/All That Is . . . There are just so many names! No wonder some, opting for simplicity rather than intricacy, want to say growth is a lonely path!

To establish a meaningful relationship with your Higher Self, we suggest that you make your own kind of sense out of this confusion.  To help you, we offer the following cursory overview.

The Conscious Mind is that part of you that you traditionally call "you." It creates the form, content, and context (the backdrop) of your current, all-powerful reality.  It is the mind that uses the raw materials and the tools and energies (techniques) available to create your own reality.

The Subconscious Mind is the guardian of the content of the inner realities that influence who you are.  These inner realities only influence — they do not control who you are.  The Subconscious is the keeper of all that information from your inner reality.

For example, what did you have the first time you ate at McDonald's? Many of you may know the answer; the information is stored in your Subconscious Mind.  What did you have for dinner on May 5th, 1982?  Most of you have no idea.  Your Subconscious knows.  It stores every piece of data that you have witnessed directly or indirectly.  Your Subconscious not only knows what you had for dinner on May 5th, 1982, it also knows what everyone else who you directly or indirectly came in contact with on that or any other day had for dinner.  This information would clutter, confuse, and eventually confound you if you held it all in your Conscious Mind, so it is stored in your Subconscious instead.

The Subconscious Mind stores, keeps, guardians this information, but, if the data is to be used, the Conscious Mind still creates the form and context of its use.

The Unconscious Mind is the guardian of the content — the information — of your other realities.  It is similar, and often confused with the Subconscious because they both guardian information.  One keeps inner-reality information.  The Unconscious keeps other-reality information. That is, the Unconscious holds all the information about what you call past, future, and parallel lifetimes.  When you do successfully have a valid past-life regression, you connect with your Unconscious Mind.  As before, it stores the information, but the Conscious Mind determines the form and context of its potential use.

The Higher Conscious Mind, which is another name for your Higher Self, is the guardian of all the information, is the keeper of all the possibilities — and we mean ALL the possibilities, not just the ones you are consciously aware of — of change, growth, transmutation, transformation, and transcendence.  Anything to do with becoming more of who you are — anything to do with becoming more of God/Goddess/All That Is— is what the Higher Consciousness is about.

Well, some of the inner-reality and other-reality information held by the

Subconscious and the Unconscious has to do with growth, doesn't it? Yes! That is why the Subconscious and the Unconscious are contained WITHIN the Higher Consciousness. A great deal that you hold consciously is also a part of your growth. That is so obvious, but it must be said. Your conscious mind is also WITHIN your Higher Consciousness — within your Higher Self.

The Higher Self is the guardian of the information. It holds the content. But you — and this is important — you choose and decide based on your thoughts and feelings as determined by your attitudes and beliefs what form and context this information will take.

Your Higher Self has all the information — absolutely ALL the information — needed and preferred to allow you to come Home. Even though it has all that information, you consciously choose when, how, and under what circumstances to receive the gift.

Life is a gift. Growth is a gift. When are you going to receive the gifts?

We do not ask when are you going to "learn" to receive. It is not about learning; it's about being WILLING TO RECEIVE. We ask: When are you going to receive the gift from your Higher Self and from God/Goddess/All That Is?

You decide. We await your decision.

Perhaps this drawing will help you see this suggested relationship.

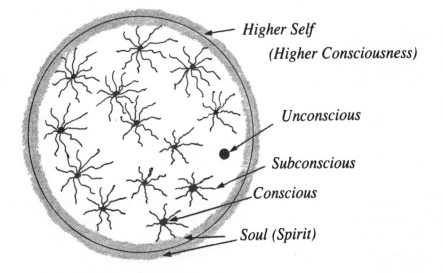

What about Soul and Spirit? The terms are used interchangeably. We suggest that the Soul is the lens to "see" your Higher Self, and it is the lens to

God/Goddess/All That Is.  As a lens, it motivates the dynamics of doing and the perceptions of being.  The Soul is that aspect of you that gives you purpose and direction.  The Soul gives you Spirit.

There was a time when you realized there was more to life than just surviving.  It was your Soul that was the spark of light — of love — that lifted you to do something about and to be different because of that realization.

In the above schematic, the Soul or Spirit is a wisp of mist just inside the Higher Self — and just beyond the Higher Self as well.  It is the lens to your Higher Self and to God/Goddess/All That Is.

We suggest this topography.  It is not the only one.  We have not said everything there is to say about any of these topics.  Our purpose here is to give you hints and clues, not to club you over the head.  Our goal is to help you grow, not to impress you with how much we know.  We work with a subtle touch . . . we speak softly.  Your relationship with your Higher Self will be much more real and unbelievably more rewarding if you will make the decisions.  Allow us to help, but you make the decisions about how it all fits together.

## *Communication, Union, Communion*

You are almost there.  You have almost finished the last step of preparation.  You are almost ready to connect with your Higher Self.  Despite your eagerness, take a moment to consider the difference between communication, union, and communion.

Communication is more than talking.  It is more than listening.  Communication involves talking and listening, and it involves a touching and changing.

Your goal is more than just talking to — or at — your Higher Self.  It is more than just listening to what it has to say.  You want to touch and change your Higher Self.  That is, you want your Higher Self to become more of what it is because the two of you are interacting.  The changes you want to allow (not make) are a result of loving, not parenting.

Additionally, you want to be touched and changed by your Higher Self.  You do not know exactly what these changes are, and you trust your Higher Self already does know.

It is not about *making* — it's about *allowing.*  Let it be.

Union is a joining together to become one.  When communication moves beyond words, you seek a union.  Ideally, when the love you have for another goes beyond words you seek a union. It may differ from relationship to relationship, but some form of union is sought when the words run out.

So with your Higher Self. You will desire to become "one with." When the teachings of any real spirituality encourage becoming "One with God," it is this union of which they speak.

Becoming one — creating union — does not mean losing your identity as some have hinted or outright said. Growth is exponential, not linear. When you grow you become *more* of who you are, not less.

When you drop a pebble into a pond, the ripple goes in all directions, not just one. When you add to your awareness, the impact is in all directions, not just linearly.

When you create union with your Higher Self, you add to who you are. The envelope, the bubble, of your Higher Self expands and you expand. Neither becomes less; both become more.

So many are confused on this point and are caught in a push-pull of growth. They sincerely want to be "one" with their Higher Self and with God/Goddess/All That Is, but the threat of lost identity prevents them from reaching that "oneness."

As with any valuable union, you become more, your Higher Self becomes more, and there is a synergy — a whole that is even greater than the sum of the two parts. Allow your Higher Self to be all that it can be. Take the responsibility and the steps necessary to allow yourself to be all that you can be. Establish communication with the intent of creating union. The synergy that results: Communion.

Communion, like the word spirituality, may have a lot of "old pictures" attached from childhood. We are not talking of partaking of the blood and flesh. More recently, the word may conjure pictures of UFO's and ET's that are up to no good. We are not talking of strange abductions and flights, real or imagined.

Communion is the resonance, the dance, created out of communication and union. It is communication, and it is somehow more. It is union, and it is something more. Communion is a oneness, and yet that does not really describe it, either.

A relationship of communion is when you give a part of yourself — a beautiful part — to your Higher Self. It is when you grow as much as you can and when you become as fantastic and as happy and as joyous as you can so that the "gift" of you that you give to your Higher Self is the best you that you have. It becomes your reason to grow. Why are you growing? Why are you evolving? So you can present the best you that you can be to your Higher Self.

Communion goes further. As well as your giving the gift of "a part of you, a beautiful part," it is when your Higher Self gives you a gift of itself, too.

It is the exchange of gifts of each other. What you will realize is that your Higher Self has been giving you its gift all along. Therefore, communion is giving the gift of you to your Higher Self and receiving the gift of your Higher Self to you that has been given all along. Communion is about exchanging the fullest gift of love. Or is it LOVE?

The Steps of Getting There . . . The Qualities of Being There . . .

Well, if you have been honest with yourself, you have taken each of the steps, and you are ready. You have taken each of the steps, and you are already there. More than being ready to begin your journey, you are already on your Sacred Journey Home.

Welcome. . .

## A Special Note

Lazaris has designed these meditations so that you can do them with total success entirely on your own. You need nothing other than Lazaris' instructions, the preparations you now have made, and the ability you already have to touch, to love, and to be loved by your Higher Self. If you would prefer that Lazaris guide you in these meditations, he has recorded them, and they are available from Concept: Synergy. You can order them by calling 213/285-1500 or 714/337-0781 or by writing to Concept: Synergy (279 S. Beverly Drive, Suite 604, Beverly Hills, CA 90212). Each meditation is 45 minutes long, and the set of all three is $24.95.

# *Part IV*
## *You and Your Higher Self*

*"The secret to successful meditation is visualization. The secret of visualizing is to know: More important than seeing with your eyes is seeing with your heart."*

*—Lazaris*

# Six

## The Meditations

**Y**ou have chosen. You know you have a Higher Self worth discovering. You understand the significance of making a viable and valuable connection with that Higher Self. Though you may not fully "grok" the precision of the relationship of all the minds and all the selves and the Soul, you have a "feel" for it. Besides, if you understand how metaphysics works, which is something you are understanding more and more, that relationship of the minds and selves and Soul is probable, flexible and fluid anyway. You have a sense of it. That's important. Finally, you can feel the subtlety and the nuance of communication, real communication with depth; of union, real union that happens inside; and of communion, giving the ultimate gift of love in your earnest search for the Love. The last step of preparation has been taken. Now the meditations.

At first, it seems extremely difficult, if not impossible, to put meditations into words. In fact, the effect can be quite enhancing. After all, it is your relationship with your Higher Self that you are looking to develop, so we encourage you to go on your meditations.

Have you ever noticed that "the book is better than the movie?" That is because what you image, what you imagine, is more pleasing to you than what other people imagine for you. That is why in a meditation we describe what to see (we even tell you ahead of time) so your imagination can work to make the experience the most meaningful for you. Some feel that we ruin the surprise factor by telling you what to expect. However, if we tell you, your subconscious and unconscious minds can more completely prepare you to maximize your experience. We are much more interested in helping you grow than we are in impressing you with surprise.

Your imagination is the best imagination for you to have. That is also why we encourage you not to share the form, content, or context of your meditations with anyone for a period of time. Then, when you do share your meditations, do so only with significant others and only share the content. Always reserve the form and context — that area over which you have conscious creative control — for yourself and your imagination.

We are about to explain the specific series of meditations that will effectively help you get in touch with your Higher Self. As we have said, no technique, be it a seven-step process or a meditation, will guarantee success. However, as you are willing, these meditations can work for you.

As with the steps of getting there, we encourage you to do the meditations in order. We suggest, though tempted, that you not proceed to the second meditation until you feel you have successfully completed the first. It may take several times. Similarly, continue working with the second until you feel secure and therefore ready for the third meditation.

You must decide for yourself; there is no one who will grade you. There is no test monitor. There is no referee. You must decide if you are ready to move on.

There is no benefit in lying to yourself. There is no value in fooling yourself. It is you and your relationship with your Higher Self that you seek, not an A+ grade or to cross the finish line first. It is not a race. It's a relationship.

"How will I know? How will I know?" you frantically ask. Once you have done the meditation you will know. It will be evidently apparent when to leave one meditation and to move on to the next.

We suggest that you read through the meditations several times first, allowing your imagination to conjure images that are significant to you. We will be clear, but if you are confused as to exactly what you are to "see," let your imagination be the guide. You see, many of the images will be archetypal; that is, though you may not really understand them, your subconscious and unconscious minds will.

Most particularly, your Higher Self wants to have you reach it. It wants you to develop this relationship you are on the brink of establishing. Your Higher Self will help you. It will not play coy or hard to get! It will help you. Will you let it?

We will cluster the images. Read the words, conjure the images as you see them, as you experience them. Additional information that can add to your understanding or the richness of the experience, but is not meant to be part of the meditation, will be in brackets [ ].

Once the images become yours, you can string them together in your memory. Some will find this easy to do. Or, you can make a cassette recording of your voice reading the words — of your voice guiding you on your journey Home. How appropriate! Or, you can memorize or say just the key words and let your imagination flesh them out, or you can remember or speak as elaborately or eloquently as you like. It is your meditation and your relationship with your Higher Self.

There are three meditations we recommend. They are called: Opening the Gate, The Doorway Home, and Love's Theme: The Touch.

## *Opening the Gate*

1.  Find a comfortable position, either sitting up or lying down. Do what you do to become relaxed.

[Some like to count down or up. Others like to drift lazily. Yet others like talking mentally to their body parts. Some find yoga postures or breathing exercises to be most effective. Do what works for you.]

2.  Once you are very relaxed, we want you to count down slowly from seven to one.

[With each descending number, instruct yourself to go deeper, to become more at ease, to relax more, to feel comfortable and safe. Instruct yourself with words that matter to you.]

3.  Find yourself in a forest. It is late afternoon quickly becoming night. The last rays of sun streak through the majestic trees. You notice the tallest trees, so powerful, so determined as they reach for the last of the sun's light. Their branches are like gnarled old fingers, reaching and stretching for the light. Then there are the shorter trees who flourish in the shade. They do not compete. They appreciate the diffused light offered by their towering friends. There are the younger trees. Some will grow to stand stately next to the tallest of the trees, and some will be more delicate, and they will be protected from the elements. Now they are young.

There is the shrubbery, tall and short, thin and stout. The harmony cradles you. There are the ferns, the ivies, the mosses. Each plays its part.

The forest floor: soft, spongy. Tiny twigs woven among the rotting leaves, the only reminder of last year's summer. The aroma is sensuously intoxicating.

You are part of the forest. You are part of its majesty. You are part of its power. You are part of its breath. Let yourself breathe. . .

Involve all your senses. Notice the colors and the shapes of this very magical forest. Listen to the gentle sounds. As you breathe, hear the forest breathe with you. Smell the luscious smells of a late afternoon forest. Touch the forest and all its love. Sense it being so real you can taste it!

[Remember, the more vivid you will allow your imagination to be, the more elegantly you will find success with meditation.]

4. Walk in the forest. Feel yourself lifting one foot. Feel the shift of weight in your hips, in your knees, in your ankles, and on your feet. As the suspended foot crunches the forest floor, hear the flutter of birds aflight and the scatter of animals afoot. Begin to walk, slowly and cautiously at first, more quickly and confidently thereafter.

5. Follow the path wherever it leads you. Let it curve this way and that. Let it gently or sharply incline or decline. Step over felled tree trunks and rocks. Lift the low-hanging bough. Follow the path wherever it leads you.

6. The night comes. Feel the dark replace the day. Sense the night coming out of its hiding places, coming out from behind the trees, from under the rocks, from behind every blade of grass. As the night comes out, let the day slip away. The night gives back . . .

[Walk and explore the forest as much as you feel is right for you. Some may only take moments and that is fine. Others of you may find yourself wandering and exploring for a long time. Take the time that is right for you. Just don't get lost. If you get bored or go to sleep, you got lost.]

7. At a certain point, the path will lead you to a clearing in the forest. There will be a beautiful campfire spitting and sputtering. The flames dance

to an unheard melody. The light beckons you. You walk into the clearing. You sit by the fire. You feel the gentle warmth of the light. You allow the darkness behind you to softly cradle you. You feel immeasurably safe.

[Take the time necessary to really let yourself feel safe. Often this feeling can be augmented by really imagining with as many senses as you can. Get lost in the imagery, not in sleep.]

8. In the flicker of the light on this dark and wondrous night, you see a gate. There it is . . . on the far side of this clearing. The fire had captured your attention so completely you did not notice until now. There, yes there it is — the Gate. Look more closely now. There on the ground — how very strange! There are four gifts! You can tell — they are gift wrapped! And, how very odd, there is one very old and very dented garbage can! Garbage can? Yes, even in the shadowy light of this very special night you can tell it's a garbage can!

9. You go to the gifts and prepare to open them all. Start with the smallest box. As you untie the bow and rip away the paper — don't bother trying to save the paper or to fold it neatly — let yourself rip into this, the first gift.

Package unwrapped, lift the lid. Inside the box is a gauze robe spun of light. It is a robe of love, light, laughter, and ease. Quickly and with flourish, put it on.

As the gentle light of love settles around you, let yourself remember why you want to love. Remember the obvious and the not-so-obvious reasons to love. Feel a beautiful urge to give, to respond, to respect. Feel a deep yearning to know. Sense the gentle tug of intimacy and commitment. Feel the rush of caring. Know that this whirlwind of emotion can provide you and those you care about —you and the world you live in — with a wonderful environment of security and pleasure, of honesty with vulnerability, with trust. These gusts of feeling can reduce your fears of loss, can let you know you are loved and cared for, and can give you the wonder of knowing that out there — somewhere out there — you have a Higher Self who loves you. You feel love. You feel loved.

[Give yourself time to feel the love — do not rush.]

10. Open the next box, which is the biggest one of all. In it you will find several things.

First, find photographs, some nicely framed, some loose, already curled and yellowed. Pictures of a past, pictures that you want to release. Take the pictures back to the fire and toss them in. Release some one at a time. Release others in handfuls. Let the fire release the past.

Second you will find an Elixir of Elegance. Drink it right down and feel a glowing warmth coming from within. Feel the elegance. There are no words.

Thirdly, you find a Gourd of Gratitude. It is shaped like a cornucopia. Drench yourself in gratitude. Feel it.

Fourthly. Find an Atomizer of Aliveness. Spritz your face. Smile with the tingle. Laugh with the tickle. Come alive!

Finally, you find a treasure chest. Within lie all the raw materials — all the choices and decisions, the thoughts and feelings, and attitudes and beliefs you could ever want. What's more, the treasure chest is almost overflowing with desire, imagination and expectation. With these gifts . . .

11.   There are more gifts. There are still two boxes remaining. The one you choose next contains . . . a tiny replica of a bridge. It is a tiny replica of a steeply arched bridge. The box contains . . . knowing. You know you have a Higher Self. You know why it is important to find it. You have some idea of where to look, and you know how to communicate, to create union, and then to find communion.

12.   The final box is also a box of knowing. As you enthusiastically tear into it, know that it contains the gift of knowing your resistance. Why are you not willing to open the gate? Eventually you will open it, but why are you not yet willing?

What are you avoiding? What is the fear?

Whom do you prefer to blame instead? Who are you punishing? Who won't you let off the hook?

What is the righteousness you hang onto?

What is the guarantee you cannot have, but insist on holding out for?

Why is your self-pity so important to you? Why is the false sense of "better than" so seductive still?

What is the sliver of the Past that you still want to relive over and over again? See what it is so you can let it go.

Open the box and see what is inside. It may be an object that is a symbol from your subconscious or higher conscious mind.  It may be a word or a picture.  You may find that there is nothing in the box, but that images are flooding your brain.  Let it be.  Just let it be.  Let it be. . . .

[Each time, what you find may be the same or different.  Have humility. Let it be what is really true for you.]

[Obviously, between meditations you will want to consciously work at releasing what stands in your way.]

13.  Now go to the garbage can and lift the lid.  It is definitely a garbage can!  Into it throw all your resistance.  Throw away what you found in the fourth gift and anything else you know stands in your way.  Especially throw away any and all feelings and thoughts that say "I don't deserve" into that garbage can.  Every little shred of fear, anger, hurt, and pity — all the bug-a-boo emotions of  worry, doubt, confusion, and anxiety.  They all go into the can.

Put the lid on and seal it.  It is done!  It is done!  It is done!  Let it be.

[Do this entire step with as much enthusiasm, with as much gusto, as you can muster.  The more feeling you can generate, the more success you are going to have.]

14.  Now go to that gate and open it.  Step through and just experience being totally ready.  Beyond the gate experience a road or a pathway.  A country road that leads somewhere.  A Sacred Road.  The Sacred Journey begins.

When you are ready, gently bring yourself out of meditation.

[Use whatever method of exit you desire.  Many like to count themselves out from one to five.  Others have their own methods.  Do what works for you.]

With eyes open, take a gentle deep breath and sharply exhale to ground yourself.  Repeat as necessary until you are grounded in your physical world.

This is a meditation of preparation.  Depending upon what you find in the last box and depending on the ease with which you were able to open the gate, you will know if you want to repeat this meditation or if you are ready to move on.  Also pay attention to how well you did with receiving the three gifts of the beginning, middle, and last steps of getting ready.

We recommend that you do this meditation at least three times even if you feel ready to move on after the first time.  If you really are ready, twice more will only reinforce your readiness.  If your negative ego is tricking you into just thinking you are ready, twice more will either allow you to be ready — thus showing your negative ego who is boss — or you will become aware that there is more work to be done.

We suggest doing this meditation no more than once per day.  If you really are in a hurry, then allow at least eight hours between these meditations.

Again, love yourself enough to be honest.

## *The Doorway Home*

1.  Find a comfortable position, either sitting up or lying down.  Become relaxed by whatever method you desire.  Once you are totally at ease,we want you to count down slowly from ten to one [not seven to one, but ten to one].  With each descending number allow yourself to become totally relaxed, feeling totally safe and secure.

When you reach the number one, you are totally relaxed, feeling gentle and at peace.  You will find yourself at the Gate.

See with your eyes or your heart the cool and peaceful night.  The firelight dazzles behind you.  The shadows dance with the flame.  The distant trees are silhouetted against the black sky.  Smell the smells of night. Hear the rhythmic sounds.  Touch the Gate.  Feel the wet of dew.  Feel the cool.

[Again, involve as many senses as you can and be as vivid with your imagination as possible.  It will improve the impact and the effectiveness of the meditation.]

2.  Push the Gate open and, without hesitation, step through.  You are on a country road.  You are on a Sacred Road.  Your Sacred Journey has begun. You are on your way to meet your Higher Self.  Feel the excitement.  Feel the joy.

Step brightly through the night and into the grey of early dawn.  Allow yourself to experience the full grace of sunrise.  See the first hint of red and the entrance of morning orange before the triumph of yellow.  Watch the dew glisten and rise in a morning mist. Hear the day begin as you walk the country road.

The Sacred Road is lined in trees. On the left is a brook. The waters roll by fast, pounding the rocks. It is a bubbling, babbling brook. On the right there are rolling hills. At a distance an old man rakes leaves. He is burning piles of leaves. They smolder. The smoke is sweet. With a steady rhythm, the old man rakes.

3. Stop and look back. See all the clutter of your past. See the ruts you once were caught in. See the gravel of pity you used to slip and slide around in. See the boulders of stubbornness. See the pot holes of struggle and guilt and pain and . . .

Look forward. Look to the future. Look to what you are becoming. You are on the way to meet your Higher Self!

Ahead of you, you see a beautiful covered bridge. It reminds you of New England, even if you have never been there. It reminds you of what you think New England ought to be like even if it isn't. As you contemplate New England you enter into the covered bridge.

Smell the wood. Damp. Feel the dark. Cool. Hear the echo of your breath. Calm. Deeper into the bridge. Darker. Totally dark. Black.

You hear footsteps! Someone is in there with you. They are walking faster and faster. Fear. You cannot see! You cannot seeeeeee! You begin to run. They are closer now. Who? What? What!

They are your footsteps! You breathe. You laugh. You stop running and walk out of the dark. You walk into the light. You are free. You are free. Ha! You are freeeeeeee!

4. In your joy, you did not see it at first. Over there, just off the road, is a temple. There. Over there, on the left. It glistens in the sunlight. It sparkles! In awe, you walk off the path, through the grass to the steps. Walk up and approach the door.

The door may be simple or ornate. Perhaps it is made of gold or maybe rough-hewn wood. Let it be what it is. The door to a temple — your temple of All Knowing.

Step through the door into the cool of marble floors and marble walls. In the center there burns an eternal flame. Bordering the circular walls are bookcases filled with all kinds of books. From ceiling to floor there are books of all shapes and sizes. The few chairs and study tables are but shapes in the shadows in the silence of the Temple of All Knowing.  High windows let in the last of the day's light.


5.  You walk quietly, yet quickly, to the flame that always burns.  You sit. Be still. . . .


[Give yourself time here just to be with yourself and with the flame and with the Temple.  You may feel as though you have been here before.  You have.  Many times.]


Be still. . .


Realize.  You have a Higher Self.  You are about to meet that Higher Self.  What fears do you want to let go of?  Give them to the flame.  What joys do you want to feel?  Receive them from the flame.

Recognize.  It is extremely valuable to you finally to meet your Higher Self. You have tried before. Now you know you are really going to meet your Higher Self.  You have been seeking this *something more* ever since you realized there was more to life than just surviving.  You are about to find a major piece of that *something more.*  Let it in.  Feel.

Remember.  Your Higher Self is like a huge shimmering bubble of possibility.  It is like a huge shimmer of light — like a huge shimmer of love. . . . or is it LOVE?  Let yourself accept.

Reach.  Know that you will begin by communication, then union.  Then you will reach for communion.  The resonance.  The dance of you and your Higher Self.  Open your mind.  Open your heart.


Be still. . . .


6.  Stand and walk around the flame to the far side of the Temple.  There is a back door.  A simple door.  Open it and step out into the night, the starry, starry night.

In the night you can see there is a hill — a gentle mound — and a second hill.  There is a soft path in the grass.  Tiny crystals grow along the pathway. They dazzle in the night, in the starry, starry night.

High in the sky over the second hill you see a falling star, a streak of light across the sky, only this falling star doesn't disappear in a flash. It lands on that second hilltop!

You move swiftly toward the light.

[See the cover for a sense of the visualization in this meditation.]

7. As you walk up the path, there is a massive geometric shape of light. It is the Way Shower, the abstraction of light that can guide you on your path — that can show you your Sacred Journey. This light is the doorway Home. As you approach this geometric of light more slowly, you see an Old Man standing there. He is gentle, filled with Love . . . or is it LOVE?

[Who is the Old Man? He is the one who knew you when . . . He is the one with the eyes that watch and guard your sleep. He is the child's sandman. He is the adolescent's dreamer. He is the witness who is always there whenever you take a giant step toward Home. Some want us to be the Old Man. We will be your Old Man, if you like.]

8. You approach the Old Man and through the tears in your eyes you see the tears in his. Through your love for him, you feel his love for you. You reach out and touch. His body is old. His face is full of wisdom lines — wrinkles. You embrace. Let go of all your tension. He will take all your woe.

[Give yourself the time you need to feel the incredible compassion and love you have. Really let yourself feel your emotion. Some people cry, but you do not have to cry. Just feel. Anyway that happens for you, just let it be real for you.]

9. Now it is time to meet your Higher Self. The Old Man will help you. To enter this geometric of light you must give a gift. The massive light will ask you for a gift.

Let the light ask. Listen for what it requests. DO NOT GIVE THE GIFT. DO NOT! Just listen.

Turn now to the Old Man and ask permission.

IF he tells you, "Yes, give the gift requested," then give the gift. Conjure it in your mind, and it will be there to give.

[His words may not be exact, but you will receive his communication and you will know.]

IF he says, "NO, DO NOT GIVE THE GIFT," do not give it! Instead ask again. Then repeat the procedure until the Old Man says, "Yes."

[You see, your negative ego can interfere, and the Old Man can help you avoid that. Also the geometric energy is pure energy. It is available to open the doorway Home, but it does not hold your personal best interest at heart. It is energy, not a consciousness who cares about you. The Old Man is. Let him guide you. Have humility. Do not think you have all the answers, because you don't! You know that, but your negative ego wants to pretend.]

10.   Giving the gift requested, the light opens for you. Alone, for the final steps you must make on your own, you enter the light. Walk and float through a glorious tunnel of light. Travel through all Time and all Space. Travel to the edge of eternity. Travel to the edge of your reality.

We will be waiting there. Welcome. . .

[We will appear as a spark of light that grows to become a vertical oval of light just as tall as you.]

Let us surround you in our light and in our love. Our love is here for you. We will never force it upon you. We will never make you accept it. We love you too much to do that. We respect you too much. Let us love you.

11.   You stand on a brink. You stand on a brink of light. Before you is a shimmering bubble of all possibility — a bubble of light — a bubble of love.

Before you is a delicate shimmer of total vulnerability. You stand. Silent. In awe. In love.

[As you might imagine the Houston Astrodome or any other huge covered arena, so visualize this bubble similarly. Only it is mammoth in size. The light stretches up and down for as far as you can imagine above and below you. It reaches to the left and to the right and out in front of you for what seems like forever. It is so huge that it takes your breath away. You stand at the end of the tunnel of light, on the brink of this shimmering bubble, and you are stunned. Speechless, you can feel the "goose-bumps."]

[Each time you do this meditation, it is important to recreate the feelings of awe and wonder. Never take your Higher Self for granted!]

You stand silently on the brink of your Higher Self. This obviously is not all of your Higher Self, but this majestic sphere of love and light is the part you can relate to.

Welcome. . .

Will yourself to center of your Higher Self and within an instant you are there.

In silence just sit and be. Just be.

[Again, give yourself time just to be still and to feel the love. Many report that a tremendous amount of burden is lifted in just this introductory silence. Many report that their lives change just from this momentary internal rapport. Give yourself a chance.]

12. Will yourself to one of the sides of your Higher Self, and you are there. Gently reach out and touch the thin skin of light. Feel how soft, how tender, how loving even the touch is.

Begin to communicate. Say, "I love you."

Feel the tingle and shudder of sheer joy as your Higher Self hears — lets in — your communication.

Listen as your Higher Self says, "I love you, more than you will know."

[In this state, your Higher Self often speaks in tones like the tones you heard in "Close Encounters of the Third Kind." It is similar, but not the same. Or it will speak in color. Either way, it communicates in undulating waves of energy.]

[Sometimes your Higher Self will communicate with voice. It will sound like a voice inside of you.  It will still come in undulating waves of sheer ecstacy.]

As your Higher Self speaks by tone, color, or voice, you are literally lifted and, like riding a crest of a wave, you are carried into sheer bliss — into an incredible ecstacy — beyond any real or imagined meditation or drug experience or out-of-the-body experience.  Be lifted beyond anything that has ever been.

All this from a simple "I love you."

13.  In the inner silence, be with your Higher Self and talk of love and intimacy.  Talk of caring and laughing.  Talk of light and laughter and joy.  Be carried by your Higher Self, as it speaks to you of love.  Touch and be touched.

Know that you are on your way Home.  Know that you are on your personal Sacred Journey.  Know that you have found you and your Higher Self.

Celebrate!

[Give yourself the time you need. Do not worry if you "run out" of things to talk about.  This is just your first or early visit.  There will be plenty of things to explore.  Your relationship has just begun.  It is growing. . . .]

14.  It is time to leave.  Will yourself to the specific edge with the tunnel of light.  By the power of your imagination, you are there.  You look back, longing.  You look back without sadness, because you can return anytime.  Now that you have found each other, neither of you will lose the other.

Say good-bye.  Turn without looking back, and move quickly through the tunnel.  Move through the geometric abstraction, the Way Shower.  Move back into the stillness of the night, into the stillness of this starry, starry night.

The Old Man waits.  He loves.

Look up into the night and see all the stars shining so brightly.  The stars are yours tonight, because you love.  Because you love.

Among all the stars there is a tiny speck of light.  There is a tiny spark of light — spark of light.  We wink at you and say, "We love you.  As long as there is light, we love you."

[Allow yourself to come out of meditation now. Some like to count from one to five. You do whatever works best for you.]

With eyes open, take a gentle deep breath and exhale sharply. Repeat as necessary to ground yourself into the physical.

This meditation is geared to get you in touch with the abstraction of your Higher Self. This visualization is closer to the actual sense of your Higher Self than a personification would be. Though you might want to see your Higher Self as a person, it is critical that you sense it in its more abstract form, too. You will have many occasions to work with your Higher Self where this shimmer of love and light is absolutely the most effective way to work with it. There will be other times that a personification is more effective. Develop both ways of experience, and you will have a vibrant relationship with this incredible part of who you are and who you are becoming, your Higher Self.

When you feel you have established the desired rapport, move on to the final meditation. Here is where you meet and touch the personified Higher Self. This the companion in growth that you have been seeking.

Though eager to move to the third phase, we encourage you to do "The Doorway Home" meditation at least seven times before moving on . . . more if you are not yet ready.

Some ways to tell if you are willing to move on:

1.  What are the gifts being asked of you by the geometric of light? Often it will ask for things you need to change or give up about yourself. It will often ask for blockages.

2.  When you reach the end of the tunnel and the beginning of your Higher Self, how effectively can you maintain the aliveness? Can you still be stunned and awed by that first view of your Higher Self? Does the vastness and majesty still grip you? If yes, then you are ready to move on.

Still, wait until you have completed this meditation at least seven times. Your patience and your persistance will pay off. Remember, the goal is not just to experience your Higher Self. You are looking for a living, breathing, loving, embracing relationship of love and work.

How many hours, how many days are you willing to give to a human friendship, to an intimate friendship, to an intimate relationship? Isn't your Higher Self worth at least that?

## *Love's Theme: The Touch*

1. Relax. Find a comfortable position, and let yourself begin to relax. Close your eyes gently and easily. Relax. Use whatever method of relaxation works best for you. Do what you do to close off the outside world and to open up your inner world.

[Give yourself enough time here. This is the third and final phase, and you can want to rush it. Don't.]

Being totally relaxed, we want you to count down from twenty-three (23) to one. With each descending number allow yourself to adjust to the appropriate resonance to allow total success. You are going to meet the personified Higher Self. Allow your subconscious and your unconscious minds to make the necessary adjustments to maximize your success. Even though you do not understand all that those minds will do, they know what has to be done to allow you total success. Begin counting now.

[The first numbers may be counted more quickly if you like. However, when you count the last several numbers allow them to be counted at an easy pace.]

2. As you are counting remember and mentally repeat: "I love myself. . . I am letting go of the past. I love myself. . . More and more, my life is elegant. I love myself more and more. . . I feel grateful. . . I feel grateful. . . I am alive. . . With raw materials and all the tools, I love myself. . . I am about to discover my Higher Self. . . I love myself."

[This does not have to be repeated exactly. The idea is to review all the steps of getting there as you are counting down.]

When you hear the number one, you will find yourself beyond the flame in the Temple of All Knowing. At the count of one you will be there.

3. Gently open the back door and step out into the night. Step out into the starry, starry night. See the soft darkness of the sky. Notice the stars like so many diamonds on the black velvet canopy of the night. Feel the quiet

cool. Sense a soft night breeze caress your cheek. Smell the hushed fragrances. Notice the dew on the grass underfoot. Become a part of the night.

A falling star streaking across the sky . . . but this falling star is different. It lands on the second hilltop and explodes into a brilliant flash. You squint, covering your eyes. Blinded by the light. Blinded by the light.

As your vision returns you see a breathtaking geometric of light. You see the Old Man waiting there. Waiting for you, he stands patiently.

Quickly, you run across the first hill and down into the valley and up the second slope to the hilltop.

[See the front cover of the book for one person's interpretation of this scene.]

Greet the Old Man. Experience, with all your senses, his intense love for you. Experience your intense love for this Old One. See the love in his eyes. Hear it in your breath. Reach out and grasp his hand — old, wrinkled, soft yet powerful, old yet vital. Feel the love. Feel the caring.

4. Turn to the light, and it will ask for a gift. Hear it ask. Now, listen. DO NOT GIVE THE GIFT. JUST LISTEN.

Turn to the Old Man and ask permission to give the gift. If he indicates permission, give the gift and continue. If he declines permission, ask the light again. Repeat this procedure until you get permission from the Old Man.

[Your negative ego may try to play one of two games. First, it may have you asking and asking over and over again. If you have to ask more than four times, stop the meditation: Your negative ego is hassling you. Try later or another day. Don't force yourself. Rather than meditate, process your ego. Get it out of the way. Second, your negative ego will tell you, "Go ahead. You don't need to ask the Old Man. The light is asking for the same gift it always asks for, so go ahead." If the light is asking for a different gift, the negative ego may tell you that you can figure it out. "You still don't have to ask," it may say. Do not listen to your negative ego.]

[Remember, the negative ego's most persistent message is: "What negative ego is Lazaris talking about? My negative ego has been handled months ago!"]

5. With permission, give the gift and pass into the light. Pass into the Way Shower. Pass into the light that guides your Journey Home. Step into the light of your continuing Sacred Journey.

Travel — walking and floating — through the light. Let yourself celebrate your success. Let yourself feel the wonder and the joy. Experience.

Notice a split in the tunnel of light. Straight ahead is the usual path through the light to your Higher Self and Home. Such longing, such yearning pulls you there. However, off in this direction there is another path to follow. From this alternative path you feel the pull of love. There is a subtle mist in this light. There is a kind of mystery and intrigue. Mostly there is love . . . or is it LOVE?

Follow this new path. Delightfully float upon the mist following the curve — following the flow up and down, left and right, curving this way and that.

6. The tunnel of light deposits you quietly in a meadow — in a meadow in the middle of the night. The stars are out tonight, and they are shining so brightly. You sit alone in the meadow. Silence.

You choose, "Tonight I meet my Higher Self. Tonight we touch. Tonight we love."

You decide, "It is so. It is so. It. . . is . . . so."

Feel the truth of your choice, of your decision. Sit with that feeling. Think about it. Do that now.

[Give yourself time here. It would be easy to skip over this step and "get on with it," but this step is critical to allowing greater success. We are not suggesting you will not be successful otherwise. No, we are saying that doing this step will enhance whatever success you are already planning to have.]

While thinking and feeling, look, over there at the edge of the meadow. There, yes, there. See a tiny speck of light, no larger than a firefly. We are waiting on the edge of your reality. We are waiting to love you. When you are ready, get up. Walk toward that tiny spark of light — that tiny spark of love. When you are ready. Let's go Home.

7.  We welcome you, and our light grows as tall as you.  We stand before you as a sphere of light, and sphere of love.  Let's walk.  Just you and us, let's walk. . . .

Without words, we walk.  The silence is filled with love.  We love you. We feel your love, too.  Thank you.  We walk.  In silence we walk.

Ahead, see a gate.  It looks familiar.  It is the gate at the edge of the clearing so long, long ago!  Excitedly you run to it.  We meet you there.  As you swing the gate wide, there is a garden there — not the road, the country road you expected — there is a mystical, magical garden there!

It is an ancient garden.  Explore.


[Give yourself the time to look at all that is here.  Again, involve as many of your senses as possible.]


The green is so lush, so rich.    And   the  splashes of color — reds, oranges, purples, and greens.  Oh, the yellows, too.  See the shapes and colors, if not with your eyes, then with your heart.  Hear the sounds of the garden. The creak of ancient trellises, held together by the vines they used to support. The hush of gentle garden breezes.  The babble of waterfalls and ponds.  Hear the garden in your mind.  Smell the intoxicating wonder that only a garden holds.  Touch the ground, the leaves, the cobblestones.  Let it be so real you can practically taste the magic of the garden.


8.  Come with us now.  We want to show you a special tree.  It is a tree of light, a tree of wisdom, a tree of excellence.  It is a tree of love.

As you see it there, you stand very, very still.  It is incredible!  It is beautiful!  It is more beautiful, more moving, than any tree you have ever seen or even imagined!

You cry inside.  You are witnessing God/Goddess/All That Is as a tree. You are seeing All That Is.


9.  Sit under the tree.  Rest.  Nestle in the gnarled roots.  Get comfortable. Rest.


[Pause.]

Sense that there is someone else leaning against the tree. On the other side. You cannot see it; you just feel it. Someone is there.

Your Higher Self is sitting there. Your Higher Self is sitting there in a human body. It may be of the same sex as you — it most often is. However, it could have taken on the form of the opposite sex. Do not presume — do not limit. Know that your Higher Self is sitting there!

Repeat: "I am worthy. I am willing. I deserve love. . . . I am worthy. I am willing. I deserve love. . . . I am worthy. I am willing. I deserve love."

10. Slowly put your hand, palm down, upon the ground. Put it out there at your side. Reach with it, and firmly place it upon the ground. Place it so it is halfway around the tree, so that it's halfway between "my Higher Self and me." If you are on one side and your Higher Self is on the other, your hand is palm down on the side that separates you from your SELF.

Feel the roots upon which your hand rests. Feel the dirt and any grass that is there. Feel the warmth of your hand firmly resting on the ground.

Then you notice. Someone has just placed their hand on top of yours! Someone has just put their hand on top — right on top of your hand! YOU CAN FEEL IT. YOU CAN FEEL IT.

Flesh against flesh, you can feel it. You can feel it. Slowly rotate your hand so your palm touches their palm. You are holding hands.

SQUEEZE. GENTLY SQUEEZE! . . . and the other hand . . . squeezes back! It is real. It is real. Let it be real!

Lean around the tree to discover each other. Look at your Higher Self. Say "Hello."

Talk now. Get acquainted. Get to know each other after all these years. After all these many, many years of thinking there was only you. After all these many, many years to discover there is another you — there is a Higher Self! Touch. Be touched. Love. Be loved.

11. Walk together now. The two of you, walk. We are waiting for you in the clearing. Come. As you enter the clearing, come sit with us. It is time to exchange the gifts.

As you are seated comfortably, you and your Higher Self are facing each other. Smile. Laugh. Love.

Your Higher Self will give you a gift. No permission is necessary. Accept the gift. It may have literal meaning. It may be symbolic. It may be an object. It many be an emotion or a thought. Accept the gift. Ask what it means. Ask. . . .

[Talking to your Higher Self is by telepathy. It will respond with telepathy. You are not saying your words "out loud," so why should your Higher Self? It may sound like your own voice, or it may sound different, but it will sound like it is inside of you. That's because it is. Let it be.]

Now your Higher Self will ask you for a gift. Rather than deciding for yourself, allow your Higher Self to ask you for what it wants from you. It may be a literal or symbolic object. It may be a promise or commitment. It may be an emotion or a thought. It may be anything, but it will never require struggle or hardship. It will never bring pain. Your Higher Self will ask you for a gift. It is a gift that you shall give.

[Allow the gift exchange, paying close attention to what is given and what is requested.]

[Always, if you do not understand, ask for clarity. It will come in words or pictures. It will come. Know that.]

12. Now the two of you stand up and take each other's hands, making a circle of two. Slowly begin to dance. Begin to dance the dance of love. Slowly the movement begins and then faster and faster you dance. You dance the dance of Love. The more you dance, the more love you feel. Spinning faster and faster, you become as one. You become as One. You feel the love, you feel the Love, and you feel the LOVE.

13. Thrilled and exhausted, you collapse laughing, hooting, and hollering. You are filled with love, light, laughter, and ease. You are filled with fun!

Catching your breath, you talk. Talk about the things you want to learn. Talk about the limitations you are overcoming or are planning to overcome. Talk about the future you are creating. Talk about the future the two of you are now going to create together.

Let yourself and your SELF talk about your dreams and plans. Share with your Higher Self. Let your Higher Self share with you.

Hear your Higher Self call you by name. Call it by name, too.

[Its name may be the same as yours, or it may be different. Do not read too much into the name. Do not play games like: "My Higher Self's name is Jesus . . . I wonder if . . .?" Please love yourself more than that. The most important thing about your Higher Self's name is that it gives you something to call them other than "Higher" or "Self" or "H.S." or "H.C." as some have done. A name is more personal. Use it. If you do not get a name, wait. One will come.]

14. Let us surround you both in the bubble of light that we are. Let us plant in each of your minds the love that you each have discovered. Let us plant in your conscious, subconscious, and unconscious minds the love you suspected and the love your Higher Self knew was there all along.

In a flash we whisk up high into the heavens. As long as there is light we will be there. As long as there is light we will love you both.

With Love and Peace. . .

Let yourself come out of meditation. Say good-bye to your Higher Self. Count yourself out.

[Sit quietly after you open your eyes. Let yourself adjust. Be still.]

With eyes open, inhale gently, hold for a moment and exhale sharply. Repeat as necessary to ground yourself.

This meditation, Love's Theme: The Touch, should be done three times — more if you like, but at least three times. Once you have completed the third time, you can contact your Higher Self in less elaborate ways.

To connect with the abstract Higher Self, always go through the Way Shower — the abstraction of geometric light — though a gift-giving is not always necessary. If you feel the need or desire to give a gift, always get permission from the Old Man. ALWAYS! When you come to the end of the tunnel of light and you are standing on the brink, always feel awe. Always feel the spine-tingling, goose-bumping thrill. ALWAYS! Never take your

Higher Self for granted. It will not punish you, but you might, and your connection will not be as strong as it could be.

To connect with the personified Higher Self, you can invite him/her into any meditation. There is no need for a formal ritual of entry. It is your relationship with your Higher Self. Be appropriate without overdoing it. Just like with any relationship, use discretion. Be loving.

You are now in touch with your Higher Self. It knows your name. You know its name.

You are well upon your way. You are well upon your Sacred Journey.

What next?

# Seven

## The Actions:
## Working with Your Higher Self

You now have a living, breathing, loving, and embracing relationship with your Higher Self. You can connect with a very real Higher Self in its abstract or personified form. Both are viable and exceedingly valuable.

You have given the gift of "you" to your Higher Self, and you have allowed yourself to receive the gift of "Higher Self" from your Higher Self.

You know about giving love. And you know about receiving love. But what about being loved? What about being loved by your Higher Self? How do you do that?

Giving love involves actively giving, responding, respecting, etc., all the way to caring so as to provide very specific and valuable feelings, feelings of security, pleasure, honesty, etc., all the way to the feelings of really being known. Receiving love is being willing to let in these specific functions and being willing to allow yourself to feel these particular feelings.

Being loved is changing. Being loved is growing and changing for no other reason than "because I am loved. I am changing because somebody loves me. I am changing because my Higher Self loves me." The key to being loved is knowing that there is nothing wrong with you. You are not changing to correct anything. You are fine — just fine — the way you are. And you are changing anyway, because someone loves you more than you knew possible. Someone — your Higher Self — loves you more than you thought you could believe.

There may or may not be "things" that you would like to change, but you are not changing them for self-improvement reasons. You are not trying to add to your Human Potential. You are not trying to become more desirable or popular or whatever. There is no specific goal — there is no anticipated reward! You are growing because somebody — your Higher Self — loves you.

It is a wonderful feeling. It is a feeling that really lets you know that you are on your spiritual path. It lets you know that you are on the Sacred Journey — you and your Higher Self are heading Home.

What do you do now that you know your Higher Self? The old Eastern tale asks: "What does the woodcutter do after he has gone to the mountaintop and found enlightenment?" The answer: "He cuts wood." You live your life.

You understand this, and what do you do with your Higher Self? How do you work with it?

## *How NOT to Work with Your Higher Self*

The most common mistake people will make is to anticipate putting their Higher Self to work. There will be those who will think they can earn a living "channeling" their Higher Self. "After all," they say, "I read the book, I did the techniques — so what if I skipped a few steps — so what if I didn't really bother doing all those steps or feeling all those feelings — I got the jist of it. I got in touch with my Higher Self. I squeezed, they squeezed, what more do you want? I am ready now. I'll put an ad in the paper and off I go! Hire a little PR and I'm set!"

You may think we exaggerate. We only wish we did! Our purpose in putting this book together is not to create more "alligator men" and "bearded ladies." Our intent is not to add to the "Carnival of Metaphysics." Our purpose is to help you, to help you become more of who you really are. You said you wanted to grow, that you wanted to evolve. We are here as a response to that request.

We also want to help you fold up some of the tents and to silence some of the nickelodeons of the metaphysical "barkers" out there. With a loving relationship with your Higher Self, you will be more able to discern, you will be more able to hear the hype, you will be more able to walk away with your own power intact.

In our example, we suggested that those who think they should put their Higher Self to work skipped some steps and did not bother "feeling all those feelings," because if they did do all the steps and if they did feel all the emotions — if they really did do the meditations as indicated — they would never even consider the idea of putting their Higher Self to work!

When you fully follow the steps, really feel the feelings, and think the thoughts, the love you feel would not lead you to these carnival-like conclusions. This is your Higher Self you are talking about!

You see, we are not the Channel's (Jach's) Higher Self. He has a powerfully loving and intimate relationship with his Higher Self. He would never consider "channeling" that energy. The relationship is too personal — too private — as it should be.

Jach did not attempt to develop a relationship with us. We came to him, so to speak. He did not plan on us, though we planned on him. We love him grandly and help him immensely, but we are not his Higher Self. Perhaps he would like us to be, but, alas, we are not.

We know there are those who claim to be able to teach you to channel. Some can. However, there is channeling and there is channeling. You must differentiate.

There is subjective channeling. Each of you can learn to channel FOR YOUR OWN BENEFIT — FOR YOUR OWN GROWTH. Each person who is creative is actually or potentially channeling at least their innate or developed creativity! When you have an inspired thought that spontaneously spills out of you, that is also a form of channeling. Many times during a day you may channel — you may channel yourself. The common denominator is that the information is FOR YOUR BENEFIT — IT IS PERSONAL AND SUBJECTIVELY FOR YOU.

Then there is objective channeling which is like the work that we and some others do. You cannot take a class or even a "home study" course to develop this form of channeling. Edgar Cayce and Jane Roberts, who were both objective channels like Jach, did not seek to do this work. On a very deep level they gave permission, of course. They did not consciously learn how to channel. They were chosen — it just happened to them.

Subjective channeling — for your own growth — can be taught. Objective channeling — for the benefit of all those who are touched — cannot be taught. Hopefully, we make ourselves clear.

Though your Higher Self is real, its purpose is to find you. Its purpose is to be in a loving relationship with you, and then, together with you, to develop a more loving relationship with God/Goddess/All That Is. Its purpose is subjective. It is intended for subjective channeling, if at all.

By developing a relationship with your Higher Self, you can channel its wisdom and insight, you can channel its love and its help. The very contact that you already have had could well be called channeling, but the key is this: FOR YOUR OWN BENEFIT — FOR YOUR OWN GROWTH.

Please love yourself enough to use this energy and this relationship correctly. Love yourself enough *not* to "put your Higher Self to work." Do not try to objectively channel this personal and private relationship. Love yourself enough.

The second mistake that many will make is to believe every word their Higher Self says from the first utterance. Unless you absolutely know you have cleared out your negative ego and have cleared your subconscious and unconscious mind of all aberrant thoughts — something none of you can say is true — you need to work with your Higher Self to develop the skill of communicating.

A common scenario: "Well, I finally got in touch with my Higher Self. I doubted myself for so long. I'd hate to think I am deluding myself. I would just die if I were deluding myself." This is an attempt at manipulating self and others so no one will even hint that you might be in negative ego spaces, and this is how the scenario begins.

It continues, "My Higher Self said that I am totally enlightened and that anyone who might question that is only seeing their own inadequacy. Anyone who disagrees is only jealous. I can quit my job because my Higher Self is going to give me money. I can stop eating because my Higher Self is going to nurture me totally. My Higher Self is going to buy me a house next week."

You think we exaggerate. We have not. Each of these statements has been made by people who skipped too many steps, numbed their way past too many emotions, and prematurely connected with what they thought was their Higher Self. In fact, they discovered ego mimicry.

Some have connected with their Higher Self legitimately and then retreated headlong into negative ego. Yet others, who did not practice, slipped silently into this self-destructive place.

The ways to avoid this pitfall:

1. Follow the steps and work with each meditation until you really feel ready to move on. Periodically repeat earlier meditations as a reinforcement.

2. Listen to what your Higher Self has to say. Believe everything that can help you and is benign. Everything that can hurt you or be malicious, check it out. If your Higher Self says to call a friend because they need your help, or to drive a different way home from work, go ahead. If the communication is shaky or wrong, there is no harm.

If your Higher Self says to quit your job or to leave your spouse, or that it has personally put money into your checking account so go on a spending spree, do not do any of it. Rather, check it out first. Perhaps each of these things is true; if so, then each can stand scrutiny.

If your Higher Self says not to check it out, but to just have faith in them, with great firmness tell your negative ego where to go. You are not talking to your Higher Self.

This varying approach to the information received will allow you to develop rapport with your Higher Self. You will learn how your Higher Self communicates with you, and your Higher Self will learn more specifically exactly how to reach you most clearly.

In time your communication will be very clear and uncannily accurate.

3. Continuously reinforce the Steps of Getting There. If you will remind yourself to love, release the past, and so forth, your communication will become clearer and clearer. Also ask your Higher Self to help you instill these seven Steps of Getting There so they are more and more the qualities of being there.

4. Remember your purpose. Remember the love you feel for your Higher Self and remind yourself of the love it has for you. Also, remember that everything you and your Higher Self do together is aimed at developing a closer, more meaningful, and more real relationship with God/Goddess/All That Is.

When evaluating the communication with your Higher Self, ask yourself if the information is a growth choice (bringing you closer to your goal), or is it a fear choice (retreating from your goal)?

Being aware of these two major mistakes can clear the way for a powerfully rewarding relationship between you and your Higher Self. Remember, your Higher Self wants to reach you, wants to love you, wants to touch you. It will more than meet you half way. Give it a chance. Give yourself a chance.

## *Seven Easy Steps*

Having cleared out the temptations to go askew, you can now see clear ways of really working with your Higher Self. Once you have connected, like the woodcutter, you will "chop wood." But you can chop your wood with a depth, with a richness, that others may not know — if you are willing. You will chop your wood more happily and more joyously — if you really desire.

As a result of this new and developing relationship between you and your

Higher Self — because you are jubilantly moving forward on your Sacred Journey — your life can reflect that love, light, laughter, and ease.

It is hard to contain success. It can spread to every area of your life! You can become an inspiration to yourself and to everyone you come in contact with — to everyone you touch.

The more willing you are, the more this (and a great deal more) can open up for you. Knowing exactly how to work with your Higher Self can augment the potentials and can stimulate the willingness. You can get excited on your own, but if you are not really sure of how to work with your Higher Self or what benefit you can derive from such work, that excitement is going to be somewhat dulled. With precise methods you can get very enthusiastic. You can come alive with a dynamic creativity — you can be filled with desires, imaginings, and expectations. You can, once again, begin to Dream . . .

We are going to suggest several ways to work. Think about each, and imagine how each can apply to you, specifically. Use these possibilities as your probabilities and as catalysts to generate additional probabilities. For it is from these probable ways of working that you will design and develop the actual ways that you will be working with your Higher Self. It is from these and other probabilities that you will sculpt your individual relationship with your Higher Self, and will define your Sacred Journey Home. The ways you work and interrelate will determine your very personal and very unique search for God/Goddess/All That Is.

1. Sit with your Higher Self. With your abstract Higher Self, go to that center and just sit. Just be together. This type of open-ended meditation can relieve and release the burden of "old wounds." When you have processed a piece of the past and somehow you just cannot let it go, go sit with your Higher Self. When you are willing to be successful, but really unsure as to whether you really deserve . . . go sit. Just be with your Higher Self. You have forgiven yourself and released the guilt, and now you need a healing. Turn to your Higher Self. In silence, allow the burdens to be lifted. Let the shadows be dissolved.

We have suggested this approach to a number of people, and they have reported sensational results. Some have found their lifetime fears just disappearing. Others have found that worry that has no foundation just goes away. Many have reported exciting miracles. They have no explanation. They just sat there being bathed in love for 20 to 30 minutes. A few hours or a few days later everything "just worked out."

You can also sit with the personified Higher Self, but this technique tends to work better — more completely — with the shimmer of love and light.

2. Seek guidance in understanding your Purpose. Each of you comes

into this lifetime with seven very specific Purposes — we call them Focuses. When you can discover them and make them a more vibrant part of your conscious decision-making process, your life can be more successful, rewarding, and much more fun.

We would suggest that when you are functioning in alignment with your Focuses you succeed — you create more precisely what you ask for and want than you do when you are out of alignment.

Go to either expression of your Higher Self and explore those Focuses or discuss how to implement them more dynamically and perceptively. Ask your Higher Self to elaborate more fully — ask it to "show" you what it is trying to say to you.

Let your Higher Self be creative. Perhaps it will give you a series of seven boxes, each containing knowledge of your Focuses. Perhaps it will be seven books, or pictures, or whispered secrets. Perhaps your Higher Self knows you prefer searching for buried treasure.

Once you have explored those Focuses, work with your Higher Self to make them more real in your daily life. Find out which ones to work with now, and how.

This particular type of guidance can go on for the rest of your life and then some. There is always more to learn and to explore. There is always more.

3. Seek guidance in your personal process and your specific programmings. Involve your Higher Self with as much of your growth as you desire. Your Higher Self will program with you; it will process with you. It can let you know if you are or are not being honest with your thoughts or feelings.

If you will allow, your Higher Consciousness will work with your conscious, subconscious, and unconscious minds to create harmony and greater cooperation.

The key here is never to take your Higher Self for granted. Involve it, but always keep the relationship special. If working together frequently is going to diminish the specialness, do two things. First, do not work frequently, yet. And secondly, figure out what the problem is and let it go. Remember the goal is to become one with your Higher Self on your way Home. If you hold a belief that "frequency diminishes love," can you see any reluctance to grow?

Some of you may find some resistance to including your Higher Self in your processing and programming. Most often this resistance is in direct ratio to your resistance to feeling gratitude!

4. Work together to create your reality. Go to the abstract Higher Self and dream your Dreams. Ask it to work from its level to help manifest your Dreams. While working with the abstract Higher Self, build your desire. Seek assistance in strengthening your imagination — allow it to be sharpened. Ask for an increase in expectancy. Permit your Higher Self to work with you to enhance your skill of reality creation and to improve the art of creating exactly what you want.

Sit down with the personified Higher Self and have lively discussions about what you really want to create. Share your purpose, goals, and plans. Ask for evaluation and let yourself receive your Higher Self's opinion of your hopes and dreams.

Your Higher Self may suggest strategies, or that you reorder priorities, or may have alternative suggestions. It may point out contingencies and considerations that never occurred to you. They may offer additional benefits that will increase your determination and your Vision.

Remember, your Higher Self is your friend. It wants you to grow. It wants you to succeed.

You know, every time you resolve to change or to grow, whether those resolutions are sincere or bravado, your Higher Self believes you and gets "all excited, filled with hope, thrilled" with your decision. When it turns out to be bravado or sincerity without follow-through, your Higher Self understands and waits for the next resolution.

You can "cry wolf" too often with people. You can never "cry wolf" too often as far as your Higher Self is concerned. You can never "cry wolf" too often. You are loved, truly loved.

5. Co-create your reality together. An important, but often overlooked fact: Before you can co-create you must be able to create.

Once you have worked with creating the reality you want, then you can work with your Higher Self to figure out together what reality the two of you want. You can involve your Higher Self in the decision-making process. You can create purposes together and then proceed to develop goals and plans of action. You can sit down together to map out strategies and priorities. Though your Higher Self has no obstacles or blockages, it can show you yours.

If you ever hear yourself say aloud or to yourself, "Well, I wanted to do it that way, but my Higher Self insisted . . ." or, "My Higher Self made me do it . . . ," then stop. You are not talking with your Higher Self. You are talking to your negative ego with mask!

Do not abandon your Sacred Journey. Just go back to the Steps of Getting There and review and realign.

6. Seek the Will of your Higher Consciousness. Your Higher Self is the guardian of the content of all your growth, evolution, transmutation, transformation, and transcendence. What are the Dreams of your Higher Self? Not what are YOUR Dreams, but what are ITS Dreams for you?

You can work either with the abstract or the personified Higher Self. Sit in the silence. Be still. Let your Higher Self dreams its Dreams for you. Listen. See. Accept.

What are the next steps of growth for you? Where should you be putting your attention? What's the next phase?

What Vision Quests should you be exploring? What Future Visions and New Quests would be best for you now? These are questions whose answers are contained in the Will of your Higher Self. Explore.

7. Discover the Will of God/Goddess/All That Is. To some this sounds frightening. It sounds like that "old-time religion that may have been good enough for them, but is definitely not right for me!" We did not say surrender your will to the will of God. We said discover what the Will of God/Goddess/All That Is really is all about.

The goal of the new spirituality is to give up neither your identity nor your will. Evolution is about expanding, not denying. Growth and the Sacred Journey are not just about seeking truth. They are about seeking the HIGHEST TRUTH. They are not about settling for any old truth. They about stretching for the HIGHEST TRUTH . . . and then continuing to search and reach for an even HIGHER TRUTH!

Through the relationship of you and your Higher Self — through the Sacred Journey which is you and your Higher Self — you can reveal the Will of God/Goddess/All That Is. Discovering that Will allows a giant step toward Home. It is a giant step toward oneness with your Higher Self and oneness with God/Goddess/All That Is.

The Divine Will is something that each of you will discover sometime on your journey Home. We will have more to say about it in "time to come." Let us say this. To any question you ask of God/Goddess/All That Is, the answer is always "YES!"

These are seven ways to work with your Higher Self. They are in order. Work with the first steps first and gently progress to the last. With success at each level, you will be prepared for the next level.

There is an "over-the-back-fence" wisdom that says that "if you are going to have a fight, pick on someone bigger than you so when you lose, you won't be embarrassed."

Well, just between you and us, when you are going to encounter an obstacle or learn something new, start with the easiest so that you are sure to win!

Take the first steps first and then progress.  Then you will surely win.

## *A Final Thought*

A major portion of our commitment to you is fulfilled in workshops, seminars, and private consultations.  A while back, we expanded our commitment by adding audio and video recordings of what we want to tell you.

The more of you we touch, the more deeply we will touch each of you.  That is our promise.

As the seminars and workshops have grown, people are amazed that the experience also grows in the level of love and intimacy.  The more of you there are to touch, the more deeply each of you is touched.

As a way to touch you more closely and more tenderly, we write to you.

Some have wondered — with the amount of information and with the detail of information that we offer in all the ways we communicate with you — if we are not putting ourselves "out of business."

Our immediate answer is:  No.

First, we are not in "the business" of taking power.  We are in "the excitement and joy" of helping you take it back.

Second, we are not "in business."  We are in love — with you.

We close.  With Love and Peace . . .

*— Lazaris*

# Appendix

*"For as long as there is light we will love you."*

—Lazaris

*These reference guides are here to remind you of the major components in each section of the book. One suggestion is to detach them along the dotted line and put them on your mirror as a daily reminder.*

# *Part I*

*What is the New Age?*

*The New Age is an Age of Humanity, an Age of Consciousness, in which:*

*1. Each individual willingly and enthusiastically accepts personal responsibility for consciously creating reality.*

*2. Each individual personally and practically comprehends that their world is a self-generated illusion that is limited only by their unique choices and decisions, their private thoughts and feelings, and their personal attitudes and beliefs.*

*3. Each individual joyously takes back his/her personal power and becomes their own master-creator in a co-creating relationship with God/Goddess/All That Is.*

*4. Each individual lovingly and celebratorily creates a World of Dominion rather than a World of Domination.*

# *Part II*

*The four initial choices of growth:*

*1.   There is more to life than just surviving.*

*2.   There is more to life than just having.*

*3.   I create my own reality.*

*4.   The something more is me, my dream, my Spirituality — my living, breathing, loving, embracing relationship with God/Goddess/All That Is.*

# *Part III*

## *The Steps of Getting There*

### *The Beginning: Love*

#### *The Obvious Reasons:*

*If you do not love yourself, you will not allow others to love you. You will not allow God/Goddess/All That Is to love you.*

#### *The Not-So-Obvious Reasons:*

*Love is a State of Being and Doing. It can fully transmute, transform and transcend energy — it is universal. Love is the only "line of communication" that reaches all the way to God/Goddess/All That Is.*

### *What To Do for Love and What To Provide for Love*

| *What To Do* | *What To Provide* |
|---|---|
| 1. Give | 1. Security |
| 2. Respond | 2. Pleasure |
| 3. Respect | 3. Vulnerability & Honesty |
| 4. Know | 4. Trust |
| 5. Humility To Be Intimate | 5. Reduced Fear of Loss |
| 6. Courange To Commit | 6. Intimacy & Caring |
| 7. Care | 7. Being Known |

# Part III
## The Steps of Getting There

### The Middle Steps

*1. Let go of the Past. Reach for the Future love NOW.*

2. Elegance

   — Desire
   — Clarify that Desire
   — Vision
   — Impeccability

4. Aliveness

   — Love
   — Trust
   — Enthusiasm
   — Expectancy

3. Gratitude
   — Thankfulness
   — Joy
   — Spontaneity

5. Inventory Raw Materials
   — Choice & Decision
   — Feeling & Thought
   — Attitude & Belief
   Sharpen Tools:
   — Desire
   — Imagination
   — Expectancy

Cut Here

# Part III

## The Steps of Getting There

### The Last Step: Communion

*1. Is there really a Higher Self to connect with?*

*2. Why do I want to connect with my Higher Self?*

*3. What's my topography?   How do the puzzle pieces fit together?*

*4. Communication + Union = Communion*

# More Information about Lazaris . . .

Photograph by Norman Seeff

## Lazaris workshops . . .

*Lazaris conducts afternoon, evening, weekend and week-long workshops on an ever-expanding variety of topics in many major American cities each year. A partial list of those cities includes: Los Angeles, San Francisco, Atlanta, New Orleans, Seattle, Houston, Washington, D. C., Chicago, Philadelphia & Tampa. If you would like to be placed on Lazaris' mailing list and be notified of workshops in your area, please call or write us at:*

*Concept: Synergy*
*279 S. Beverly Drive, Suite 604, Beverly Hills, CA 90212*
*714/337-0789, 213/285-1507*

## Lazaris Audio & Video Tapes

*A complete list of Lazaris' audio and video tapes is on the following page, with an order form for ordering by mail. If you wish to order by phone, please call:*

*714/337-0781 or 213/285-1500*

# LAZARIS TAPES

All of these audio and video tapes are available from Concept: Synergy by calling 714/337-0781 or 213/285-1500 or by mail by using the order form on the following page.

## VIDEOS $59.95 (VHS & BETA)

Awakening the Love
Forgiving Yourself
Secrets of Manifesting What You Want
Personal Power & Beyond ...
Achieving Intimacy & Loving Relationships
Unconditional Love
Releasing Negative Ego
Unlocking the Power of Changing Your Life
Spiritual Mastery: The Journey Begins
Personal Excellence
Developing a Relationship With Your Higher Self
Mysteries of Empowerment
The Future: How to Create It
Secrets of Manifesting What You Want, Part II
Overcoming Fear of Success
Listening to the Whispers
Developing Self-Confidence

## LAZARIS DISCUSSIONS $29.95

On Releasing Anger/On Releasing Self-Pity
On Releasing Guilt/On Receiving Love
Healing & Releasing Hurt/Keys of Happiness

## LAZARIS BOOKS $9.95

The Sacred Journey: You and Your Higher Self
Interviews with Lazaris—Book 1
Interviews with Lazaris—Book 2
Lazaris: A Spark of Love ($5.95)

## THE RED LABEL SERIES $29.95 (MEDITATIONS)

Reducing Fear & Worry/Stress
Self-Confidence/Awareness
High Engery/Enthusiasm
Happiness/Peace
Reduced/Improved Sleep
Personal Power/Dominion
Productivity/Impeccability

## OTHER MEDITATION TAPES

Cleaning Chakras/Pituitary-Pineal Meditation **$19.95**
Beyond the Threshold/Editing the Film **$19.95**
The Goddess Series, Part 1 **$29.95**
The Goddess Series, Part 2 **$29.95**

## LAZARIS & PENY TAPES $14.95

April 1986 Evening with Lazaris & Peny
July 1986 Evening with Lazaris & Peny
November 1986 Evening with Lazaris & Peny
S.F. March 1987 Evening with Lazaris & Peny
L.A. March 1987 Evening with Lazaris & Peny

## CALENDARS

Lazaris/Gilbert Williams 1988 Calendar ($9.95)

## PERSONAL GROWTH TAPES $24.95

Healing/Nature of Health I
Healing/Nature of Health II
Secrets of Spritually I
Secrets of Spritually II
Loving
Being Loved
Crystals: The Power & Use
Busting & Building Ego
Programming What You Want
Crisis of Martyrhood
Intimacy
Magick of Relationships
Earth Energy/Earth Power
The Unseen Friends
Busting & Building Image
Consciously Creating Success
Responsibility & Freedom
Excellence
Tapestry of Success

Power of Dominion
Positive Ambition
Gratitude
Mysterious Power of Chakras
Secrets of Manifesting (Audio)
Fear: The Internal War
Discovering Your Subconscious
With Love and Peace
Developing Self-Confidence
Conquering Fear
Ending Self-Punishment
Harmony: The Power Vortex
Balance: Releasing the Full Self
Abundance & Prosperity: The Skill
Abundance & Prosperity: The Art
Freedom: Its Mystery & Power
Inner Peace
Ending Self-Sabatoge (Available Nov. 1)
Harmonic Convergence: The Ritual of Emergence

# LAZARIS TAPES
# ORDER FORM

_____
NAME

_____
ADDRESS

_____
CITY · STATE · ZIP

_____
PHONE #

☐ *PLEASE ADD MY NAME TO THE MAILING LIST:*

| Qty. | Tape Title | Price |
|---|---|---|
|  |  |  |
|  |  |  |
|  |  |  |
|  |  |  |
|  |  |  |
|  |  |  |
|  |  |  |
|  |  |  |
|  |  |  |
|  |  |  |

*VISA, MASTERCARD, AMEX, Accepted*

_____
*Charge Card Number-Exp. Date*

_____
*Signature*

Money Order & Charge
Card orders shipped
within 1 week, CA
checks held 7 days
out-of-state checks
held 21 days

10.00 charge for
returned checks.

| | |
|---|---|
| SUBTOTAL | |
| 6.5% Tax CA Res. | |
| 5% Postage 15% overseas ($1.00 Minimum) | |
| TOTAL | |

## CONCEPT: SYNERGY

714/337-0781
213/285-1500

279 S. Beverly Dr.
Suite 604
Beverly Hills, CA 90212

***The Sacred Journey:*** *You and Your Higher Self.*